Cornerstones
for Writing

Teacher's Book
Year 6

Alison Green, Jill Hurlstone,
Diane Skipper and Jane Woods

Series Editor
Jean Glasberg

CAMBRIDGE
UNIVERSITY PRESS

Contents

Introduction

'Write about something you did in the holidays.' As most teachers know, this kind of instruction usually leads to uninspiring results: unstructured writing with no clear beginning or ending, which is often repetitive or a mix of fact and fantasy. Even worse, it can lead to blank sheets of paper and demoralised children. *Cornerstones for Writing* provides both teacher and children with the guidance they need to proceed step by step, with confidence, to a written text. It fully supports the writing objectives in the National Literacy Strategy.

In many classrooms, excellent work is being done to help children write fluently and effectively. However, for all too many children, success in writing continues to trail significantly behind that in reading. This resource aims to narrow the gap between reading and writing ability in a number of ways:

- by providing carefully selected texts as models, so that children learn the benefits of reading as authors and writing as readers;
- by helping children to identify key structural and linguistic features of important text types;
- by taking children step by step through the processes used by successful writers;
- by motivating children through establishing a clear audience and purpose for writing.

Cornerstones for Writing components

The resource has the following components:

Writing Models OHT Pack *or* Poster Pack

The OHT pack contains 32 overhead transparencies, which can be used with any overhead projector to display texts to the whole class. As an alternative, the same material is available in a poster pack of 16 double-sided A1 posters, in a 'write-on-wipe-off' format. Both the OHT pack and poster pack comprise:

- example texts from a variety of sources, which provide models for each of the different types of writing covered within the resource;
- versions of planning frameworks which appear in the copymasters, allowing the teacher to model planning with the whole class;
- where appropriate, activities for the whole class which draw attention to particular features of writing.

Notes on how to use each OHT or poster can be found in the instructions for each session within this teacher's book.

Teacher's Book

The teacher's book contains:

- notes to help you conduct the shared sessions for each step of the writing process; these are arranged in six units of work, covering the year;
- summaries of the group or independent follow-up activities, most of which are set out in the pupil's book (see below);
- suggestions for a guided focus for each group session ('guided group support');
- photocopy masters for group work;
- homework suggestions to support each unit;
- self-assessment sheets to allow children to evaluate their success with each unit;
- facsimiles of the text extracts in the OHT pack/poster pack, to help your planning.

Pupil's Book

The pupil's book provides activities to follow up and reinforce the teaching in the shared sessions. Most of these activities relate to the early stages of the writing process (i.e. Modelling – see below), as once the writing is well under way the children will be focusing on their own compositions.

Key to symbols	
red	activities appropriate for the less able child
blue	activities appropriate for the average child
yellow	activities appropriate for the more able child
	activities appropriate for pair or group work (speaking and listening opportunities)

Five steps to writing

For children to write confidently, they need to be taught a generic procedure which they can apply to any writing task. The *Cornerstones for Writing* five-step process helps young authors to approach their writing just as a skilled adult would. These five steps are outlined below:

1 Modelling

This step provides children with a successful 'how to' model for constructing their own text. Using the appropriate model text(s) from the OHT or poster pack, you should demonstrate how to map out a structural framework and identify linguistic features. Subsequent group activities encourage the children to remember and use this model for their own future writing.

2 Planning

Planning is an excellent method of establishing and keeping control. If children know how to plan in detail, and have practised the skill frequently enough for it to become familiar, they are likely to write more effectively.

Planning frameworks are helpful for children of most ages and abilities, especially when using one that has been problem-solved in class from a model text. Over a number of units, the children will learn the generic skill of 'finding' a suitable framework for writing and then using it to organise content. This is much more useful than becoming over-reliant on published 'writing frames', which, when used without real understanding on the part of the children, may leave some to flounder when the frame is taken away.

3 Drafting

Drafting is the process of getting words and ideas down on paper in provisional form, without worrying too much about elegance of expression or organisation of the pages. With the planning already done, the children are free to concentrate on the writing itself.

4 Revising and editing

Revising focuses on the content and style of a text, and allows the children to check that they have written everything that needed to be written, and are satisfied with it. It also provides an opportunity to evaluate the text from the viewpoint of the intended reader, and make any changes necessary to address the reader's needs. Editing focuses on accurate spelling and punctuation, to ensure effective communication of the author's ideas to the reader.

This step usually requires the most diplomatic handling by the teacher. The children have worked hard to produce their texts, and sometimes fail to see the point of doing any more work. It is very important, therefore, to show how improvements can be made. This will be facilitated by frequent reading and re-reading aloud to bring out 'before and after' contrasts. A really successful shared experience of revising and editing will often convert young writers away from a haphazard 'one-go' approach.

5 Publishing

Publishing is the final step in the process, where the text is produced in the form in which it will reach its intended audience. This may be done by, for example, the posting of a letter, the performance of a poem or the creation of an attractive classroom display. At this stage the arrangement of words on pages and the inclusion of illustrations, diagrams and other displayed material become most important.

Ensuring that the finished text reaches its intended audience in polished form validates the whole process. Even under great pressure of time, teachers ignore this at their peril! If the children's work never reaches an audience beyond their teacher, it is hardly surprising that they do not become audience-aware, and do not learn to craft texts for a variety of audiences and purposes. Young writers are often inspired by the pride and success they feel when they see their work word-processed, or neatly copied and displayed.

Teaching the five steps

Modelling

Conducting a shared modelling session

The nature of a shared modelling session is specific to each different text type, so much more detailed guidance is given in the shared session notes for each unit.

Modelling in group work

The children use a range of activities in the pupil's book and, where appropriate, on copymasters to familiarise themselves with the structure and features of the text type.

Planning

Conducting a shared planning session

Before the writing begins, it is essential that children know for whom they are writing, why they are writing, and how the outcome of their work will be 'published'. Where possible, share these decisions with the children to enhance motivation. Give them a deadline for producing the texts, tell them how much time and support will be available and whether they should write individually, in pairs or in groups.

Purpose and audience are crucial to the content, tone and length of the final document. Spend some time discussing and considering the needs of the audience: make preliminary decisions about how complicated the vocabulary can be, how formal the tone should be, etc.

Establish the intended method of publication. (This is for the children's independent writing – although the class text could also be published if you wish.) For example, the finished writing could be:

- made into a booklet for younger children;
- published in the school magazine;
- made into a classroom display;
- typed up as a letter to a specific recipient;
- read out in assembly.

Make brief notes of your decisions on these issues and keep them on display to refer back to during the writing process. Plan the shared text together with the children and, similarly, display the class plan as a model for their own plans.

Planning in group work

The children follow the same procedure as in the shared session, and plan their own texts. They work from either planning frameworks on copymasters or prompts in the pupil's book. It may be helpful to conduct a guided group session for this step with the less able children. This will ensure that they have a firm basis to work from once drafting begins (see **Guided focus suggestions** on page 10).

Drafting

Conducting a shared drafting session

It is strongly recommended that drafts be written on large sheets of paper so they can be kept for subsequent revising, and examined again alongside the finished text. It is often helpful for children to see the entire 'evolution' of a piece of writing.

Especially in their early experiences, it is difficult for young writers to be disciplined enough to stick to a plan. Read back each section of planning notes to the children as you go along and involve them in composing sentences to build and elaborate the text. Keep them firmly on track by referring repeatedly to what they have already decided to do, rejecting suggestions that would move away from this. (Occasionally, however, you may wish to add in an inspired 'extra' to make the point that, although planning is a very useful procedure, texts are not set in stone until published.)

Drafting may sometimes be slow to gain momentum – you may need to suggest some alternatives for discussion. Children often love to vote on the best choice from a number of strong suggestions. Good ideas which are not used in the shared text can be used in the children's own writing.

When drafting, do not worry about some sentences being too informal, or about words that do not quite fit – you need some material for improving in the revising and editing step. Often, if there are too many conflicting ideas, or if the children are becoming bogged down in how to write a particular part of the text, it is best to scribble something provisional and move on quickly. Problems can be underlined and returned to later. Often the solution to a writing problem becomes clearer as the text progresses.

Keep reading the text back to the children so that they establish a 'feel' for its tone and flow. Young writers often need to hear their writing read aloud in order to appreciate fully its length, sentence structure, etc.

'Time out' discussions may help to promote the full involvement of all the children during shared sessions. The use of small wipe-off boards for children to write and show their contributions may overcome any reluctance to speak aloud. It may also help to maintain pace in a lesson – especially if the children can be kept thinking and writing while you scribe an agreed sentence.

Finally, remember that the teacher is in charge of the shared text! Do not be afraid to 'drive' or control the piece to make a point or fulfil an objective. Explain and discuss how you are thinking as you work. As children gain in experience and confidence you will undoubtedly wish to involve them more collaboratively at times, but shared writing remains the main vehicle for teacher demonstration of writing skills.

Drafting in group work

It is often a good idea for the children to work in pairs and to tell their partner what they intend to write before writing it down. Verbalising their thoughts first can help the writing process and deters the children from making assumptions about the knowledge of the reader. Their partner will inevitably ask 'Why?', 'How?' and 'When?' if things are not clear to them.

It may be helpful to conduct a guided group session for this step with the less able or average children. These children will need some support with 'getting the language flowing' for a specific text type or audience (see **Guided focus suggestions** on page 10).

Revising and editing

Conducting a shared revising and editing session

Display the first draft. Discuss its effectiveness in relation to the main features of the text type, the original purpose for writing, the intended audience and so on. Praise its strengths, but be realistic about any problems or weaknesses. Remind the children that even professional authors have to revise and edit their work in order to make it worth publishing.

Straight away, deal with any parts of the text that were marked 'to come back to' while the first draft was being written. Use a new colour of pen so that changes are obvious. Next, ask the children to check the class plan and any additional materials (such as posters made in previous sessions) to ensure that the content includes everything that was planned. Discuss whether any additional content is needed at this stage. Then examine the style, flow and tone of the text. Decide whether the right words have been used, and whether any sentences need to be altered.

Sometimes a class will stoutly deny that there are any improvements to be made. Be prepared with two or three points that you are going to insist that they address. Also, be prepared to suggest some alternative improvements for them to evaluate and select from. Gradually, as they gain faith in this part of the process, the children will become more enthusiastic and discerning in their contributions.

You should also consider how well the text addresses the needs of its intended audience. Encourage the class to pretend that they are reading the work for the first time, 'in role' as members of this audience. Help the children to appreciate that a piece of writing is effective only if the intended audience can read or understand it.

Make a final check of spelling and grammar. Decide beforehand, according to your teaching objectives, how much responsibility you expect the children to take for ensuring the final standard of correctness in the shared text. Often it will be you, as scribe, who automatically assumes most editorial responsibility. Having made any necessary teaching points, remaining corrections should not take up too much time.

It can sometimes be very useful to use one of the children's drafts for a shared revision session. Children are often pleased that their work is being held up as an example (it is, of course, important to praise the work before revising and editing begins). Type out the child's work in advance, correcting any spelling, punctuation or other errors that are not to be part of the revising focus.

Revising and editing in group work

In groups, children 'echo' the revising and editing process, as for the other steps. It may be helpful to give them a checklist of questions that they can work through in pairs. For example:

- Is the language right for a report (or whatever text type is being written)?
- Are the information and the language right for your audience?
- Read your text to your partner. Is there anything that doesn't sound right?
- Have you checked the spelling, punctuation and grammar?

It is often useful to give children a <u>very specific</u>

focus for their revising and editing, and then ask them to work on this in pairs. One way the children can do this is to swap texts, and 'mark' their partner's work with some useful suggestions based on the given focus, using a different coloured pen. They then pass back the text, explain their suggestions and work together on improving the text.

It may be helpful to conduct a guided group session for this step with the more able children. They often learn best when spotting weaknesses in their own work and considering a range of possible improvements (see **Guided focus suggestions** on page 10).

Publishing

Conducting a shared publishing session

Time pressures will mean that it is easier to 'publish' some shared texts than others. Where it would be difficult to publish a complete version, pick out instances in the shared text which could benefit from presentational changes.

Remind the children of the intended audience, and any needs or preferences this audience may have. Revise the original purpose for writing, and consider how both of these factors have dictated the form the text has taken. Try to evaluate the impact the text will have on its intended audience.

Discuss the layout of the text. Identify ways in which its presentation could support the content. For instance, clarity of information in a report text could be enhanced through the use of a main title and headings, together with an annotated diagram, or a story could be illustrated in an attractive and informative way. Consider different ways of positioning the illustrations, rather than simply having the text at the top and a picture at the bottom. For example, split the text with the illustration in the middle, or put the text in a column with pictures down the side or decorative borders around the edge.

Discuss briefly the relative merits of highlighting effects such as bold, underlining, italics, enlarged font, changed font, upper case, etc. Decide how to present the title and headings.

Decide on the necessary publication methods and materials. These could include the use of a computer to produce the finished text, or some good handwriting pens and some attractively coloured paper. Using very simple paper-folding techniques, attractive 'books' can be made for the presentation of shorter texts. Despite their simplicity these often encourage children to produce outstanding results.

Publishing in group work

Once again, children can 'echo' the publishing ideas discussed and tried out in the shared session. When the children work on the 'best' copy of their work, it is a good opportunity to consider the importance of clear handwriting and good spelling.

Do everything possible to involve the children in presenting their finished texts to the intended audience, whether this entails them reading their stories to another class, performing their work in school assemblies or producing questionnaires asking other children what they think of work on display in the corridors.

How to plan with *Cornerstones for Writing*

In each year there are six units, corresponding roughly to six half-terms. Each *Cornerstones for Writing* unit takes one text type as its main focus, based on NLS requirements.

It is recommended that each unit be covered over a two-week period of concentrated, writing-focused work, as follows:

Week 1: reading linked to writing;
Week 2: writing.

To accommodate this in the teaching programme, reading and writing objectives for a chosen text type can be blocked together and given a heavier-than-average weighting of teaching time. This can include both literacy hour time and 'other English' time. Most teachers would agree that time beyond the literacy hour is essential in order to fulfil the requirement to teach extended and developed writing. Any remaining NLS writing objectives for each half term are covered in the 'additional sessions' (see below) which follow each unit.

Half term	
Week 1	Work on NLS range of texts for term and (mainly) reading objectives
Week 2	
Week 3	
	Cornerstones for Writing
Week 4	Reading linked to writing
Week 5	Writing
Week 6	As for Weeks 1–3

Each unit leads to the production of developed texts on two levels:

1. by the whole class, done in shared sessions with you, the teacher;
2. by individuals or groups, independently or with your guidance.

Over the course of a unit, you will address and reinforce many text-, sentence- and word-level objectives for the term. Once each unit is under way, particularly in the latter stages of drafting, revising and editing, and publishing, you will probably need to 'flex' the structure of the literacy hour to allow for a 'writing workshop' approach.

Whole-class work could be devoted to shared planning or writing, but incorporating supportive sentence- or word-level focuses. Guided support could focus on scaffolding the children's own work as it progresses; independent sessions should allow time for the children to plan, draft and improve their work in the light of what they are learning about the target text type. However, if you wish to follow the classic structure of the literacy hour, a unit could even be followed through in quarter-hour stages, as long as the children's interest is maintained.

It is strongly recommended that plenary sessions be maintained, even where the literacy hour has been 'flexed', in order to sum up and reinforce the children's learning during the course of each writing lesson. In this way, the children discuss not only what they have done, but also how they have done it, and what they have learnt about the writing process.

Linking reading and writing objectives

As reading and writing are inextricably linked and mutually supportive, every unit includes close reading analysis of simple model texts. However, it is also strongly recommended that each unit be immediately preceded by further reading experiences within the target text type, in accordance with NLS reading objectives. If, as the children read, they are helped to appreciate how an author has written the text with great care in a particular way and for a particular purpose, it is far more likely that they will be able to write successful texts of their own.

Using the additional sessions

As outlined above, *Cornerstones for Writing* focuses on one main text type per unit (therefore per half term), covering a great many of the writing objectives within the NLS framework. The 'additional sessions' will help you cover the few remaining objectives.

The additional sessions usually consist of a single shared session (or occasionally two or even three sessions) followed by group activities. This is because, assuming that the main text type has been taught in the way we suggest, you will probably plan to give these objectives 'light touch' treatment because of time limitations. However, the content of these sessions varies, and you should use your professional judgement in planning whether/when and how to use the following types of additional session:

- short, one-off tasks which could reasonably be achieved in a single literacy hour session (e.g. **Summarising** in unit 1);
- more broadly based objectives which you may wish to expand if time permits (e.g. **Keeping a reading journal** in unit 5);

- useful skills work which could be slotted into the main two-week writing block if you feel the children are ready for it, or perhaps taught in a guided session to one ability group (e.g. **Descriptions from different perspectives** in unit 2).

Special features of *Cornerstones for Writing*

Differentiation by colour coding

In *Cornerstones for Writing*, group follow-up activities are differentiated at three levels. Colour coding is used for this in the pupil's book and referred to in the teaching notes. The following coding is used:

- **red** to indicate activities appropriate for the less able child;
- **blue** to indicate activities appropriate for the average child;
- **yellow** to indicate activities appropriate for the more able child.

Guided focus suggestions (see below) are provided in the teacher's book for each session, with different suggestions for each of the red, blue and yellow groups. Additional differentiation can be achieved through the size and constitution of specific groupings. For example, less able or less prolific writers could be supported by allowing them to work collaboratively on one text, in pairs or groups. More able writers could be challenged to produce individual documents.

Guided focus suggestions

Group work allows small groups of children to use for themselves writing skills previously demonstrated and trialled in shared sessions. In guided group work, the demands on children's developing authorship can be carefully structured and focused by the teacher to ensure appropriate differentiation and maximum progress. The teaching notes in this book provide specific suggestions for guided group support at each stage, to help you to achieve this. However, it is of course vital to tailor your focus to the specific needs of the children in each group, which you are in the best position to assess and which no book can fully provide for.

Once writing workshops get under way (see **How to plan with *Cornerstones for Writing*** above) and the emphasis begins to shift from demonstration towards independent writing, you may choose to 'squeeze' the usual half hour of whole-class work down to twenty minutes (the plenary may also be contracted). This creates time for two guided group lessons during each workshop hour, meaning that each group has two teaching visits over the course of a week.

Speaking and listening symbol

Regardless of whether the children carry out their follow-up work individually, in pairs or in groups, it is important that they interact with one another. Specific opportunities for speaking and listening are emphasised in *Cornerstones for Writing* with a special symbol (two talking heads). This appears in the pupil's book next to relevant activities, and is repeated in the summary of activities in the teacher's book.

Structured or focused talk about writing is almost more important than the writing itself because it involves children in thinking about how to write and transmitting ideas. Although teachers sometimes worry that insufficient 'evidence' of writing activity may be produced, the finished texts at the end of each unit should reflect all the teaching and learning that have taken place.

Self-assessment sheets

Cornerstones for Writing encourages children to evaluate their own work and become aware of their progress. A simple self-assessment sheet is provided with each unit, which can be given to each child once they have completed their writing. The sheets may prove suitable for inclusion in records of achievement.

Homework

Many schools now provide regular homework for their pupils, so we include a variety of suggestions at the end of each unit. The suggestions are intended to reinforce the knowledge and skills gained in each unit, though they are not essential to the success of the writing project. To avoid any potential 'paperchase' problems – and to prevent marking overload! – many of the homework suggestions are based on research or involve reading or discussion.

Cross-curricular links

One of the main aims of the NLS is to promote the cross-curricular applications of literacy skills, rather than to teach them as simply 'English'. For instance, if the children are learning how to write reports, a real purpose for report-writing may be found in the science curriculum – the children could present, in a report, all the information they have learnt about materials, life processes, etc. Likewise, children can deploy their recount skills in history lessons, writing 'in role' as eyewitnesses to major events. You should seek cross-curricular links for writing projects wherever possible.

Clear opportunities for cross-curricular links with *Cornerstones for Writing* are highlighted in the teaching notes.

ICT opportunities

ICT will prove particularly valuable in recording, revising and editing class or individual texts. Word-processing offers a quick, easy way of finding and correcting mis-spellings or experimenting with the structure of sentences. Paragraphing, headings and the shape and size of layout can all be changed at the press of a button.

The internet used in researching information is also a powerful tool that can help children plan their writing. Where appropriate, opportunities for using the internet are clearly highlighted in *Cornerstones for Writing*.

Preparing for the National Tests (SATs)

Children will learn important writing skills in the course of their *Cornerstones for Writing* projects. These will stand them in good stead for tackling the full range of National Test writing tasks with confidence and effectiveness.

It is important for teachers and pupils to be aware that annual reports on children's performance in the writing tests commonly refer to:

- weaknesses in adapting text for different purposes and audiences, including choosing an appropriate text type and style;
- poor control over textual structure and balance – being able to select, sequence and shape events or ideas;
- problems using paragraphs accurately and appropriately;
- lack of writing 'stamina' – the tendency to lose control, slacken pace or 'dry up' before the end;
- weak or inappropriate endings, reflecting poor planning beforehand;
- poor sentence control – the ability to use and organise sentences of varying length and structure.

Teachers often feel that pupils perform at less than their best due to 'exam nerves' or through not knowing what examiners are looking for in response to particular questions. To help overcome this, *Cornerstones for Writing* provides a section entitled 'How to write answers to SATs questions' (teacher's book pp. 116–122, pupil's book pp. 68–75) which gives practice in this essential preparation.

We suggest that you use the materials provided as follows:

i Choose a question from those offered in the pupil's book, and ask the children to read it carefully.

ii Children should work in pairs to identify the writing skills the question demands, before planning how best to construct their text. They should use the questions on page 68 of the pupil's book as a guide.

iii If you wish, ask each pair to compare their findings with another pair and come to an agreed plan of action.

iv Go through the 'answers' together as a class or group. You can use the completed tables on pages 116–122 of this book as a guide.

v You may wish to ask the children to write full responses to the question. If so, remind them to show off all they have learnt about the particular text type, and emphasise the importance of sticking to their plans.

Note: this section contains facsimiles of OHTs/posters which do not also appear as copymasters.

3

Treasure Island

The captain spun round on his heel and fronted us; all the brown had gone out of his face, and even his nose was blue; he had the look of a man who sees a ghost, or the evil one, or something worse, if anything can be; and, upon my word, I felt sorry to see him, all in a moment, turn so old and sick.

"Come, Bill, you know me; you know an old shipmate, Bill, surely," said the stranger.

The captain made a sort of gasp.

"Black Dog!" said he.

"And who else?" returned the other, getting more at his ease. "Black Dog as ever was, come for to see his old shipmate Billy, at the 'Admiral Benbow' inn. Ah, Bill, Bill, we have seen a sight of times, us two, since I lost them two talons," holding up his mutilated hand.

"Now, look here," said the captain; "you've run me down; here I am; well, then, speak up: what is it?"

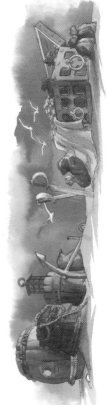

From *Treasure Island* by R.L. Stevenson

© Cambridge University Press 2001

1

Treasure Island

"Bring a torch, Dick," said Silver, when my capture was thus assured. And one of the men left the log-house and presently returned with a lighted brand.

The red glare of the torch, lighting up the interior of the block-house, showed me the worst of my apprehensions realised …

… The parrot sat, preening her plumage, on Long John's shoulder. He himself, I thought, looked somewhat paler and more stern than I was used to. He still wore the fine broadcloth suit in which he had fulfilled his mission, but it was bitterly the worse for wear, daubed with clay and torn with the sharp briers of the wood.

"So," said he, "here's Jim Hawkins, shiver my timbers! dropped in, like, eh? Well, come, I take that friendly!"

And thereupon he sat down across the brandy cask, and began to fill a pipe.

"Give me a loan of the link, Dick," said he; and then, when he had a good light, "That'll do, lad," he added; "stick the glim in the wood heap; and you, gentlemen, bring yourselves to! – you needn't stand up for Mr Hawkins; *he'll* excuse you, you may lay to that. And so, Jim" – stopping the tobacco – "here you were, and quite a pleasant surprise for poor old John. I see you were smart when first I set my eyes on you; but this here gets away from me clean, it do."

To all this, as may be well supposed, I made no answer. They had set me with my back against the wall; and I stood there, looking Silver in the face, pluckily enough, I hope, to all outward appearance, but with black despair in my heart.

From *Treasure Island* by R.L. Stevenson   © Cambridge University Press 2001

Note: this section contains facsimiles of OHTs/posters which do not also appear as copymasters.

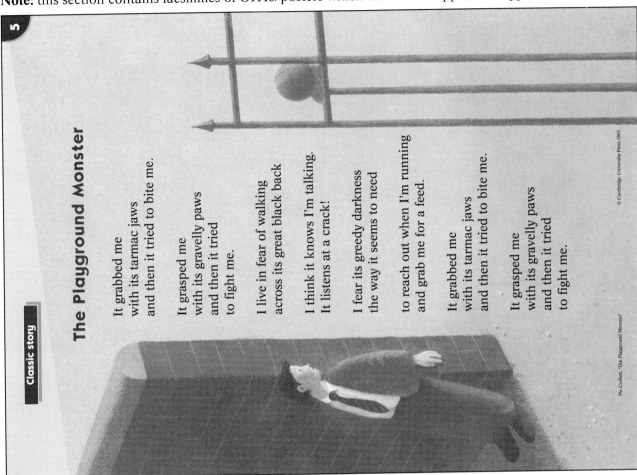

5

Classic story

The Playground Monster

It grabbed me
with its tarmac jaws
and then it tried to bite me.

It grasped me
with its gravelly paws
and then it tried
to fight me.

I live in fear of walking
across its great black back

I think it knows I'm talking.
It listens at a crack!

I fear its greedy darkness
the way it seems to need

to reach out when I'm running
and grab me for a feed.

It grabbed me
with its tarmac jaws
and then it tried to bite me.

It grasped me
with its gravelly paws
and then it tried
to fight me.

Pie Corbett, 'The Playground Monster'

© Cambridge University Press 2001

4

Classic story

Treasure Island

The three fellows must have been watching us closer than we thought for, as we soon had proved. For, coming through the narrows, we had to lie very near the southern point, and there we saw all three of them kneeling together on a spit of sand, with their arms raised in supplication. It went to all our hearts, I think, to leave them in that wretched state; but we could not risk another mutiny; and to take them home for gibbet would have been a cruel sort of kindness. The doctor hailed them and told them of the stores we had left, and where they were to find them. But they continued to call us by name, and appeal to us, for God's sake, to be merciful, and not to leave them to die in such a place.

From *Treasure Island* by R.L. Stevenson

© Cambridge University Press 2001

14

Note: this section contains facsimiles of OHTs/posters which do not also appear as copymasters.

J.K. Rowling: a biography (continued)

A few years later, at the age of 26, she moved to Portugal to teach English. Whilst there, she met and married a local journalist and their daughter Jessica was born. After two years she returned to Britain where she began to write *Harry Potter and the Philosopher's Stone*. However, it was a difficult time struggling to bring Jessica up alone. As her flat was cold and damp, she sat in cafés in order to keep warm, writing the story in a notebook and making one coffee last for two hours! Unfortunately, after all this, her ideas were rejected by a number of publishers. Eventually, however, Bloomsbury Publishing Plc, seeing the potential, turned it into a worldwide success.

J.K. Rowling's ability to hold her readers spellbound and eagerly awaiting the next book has a lot to do with her skills as a storyteller. However, does Harry Potter's biggest battle lie ahead? How will he stand the test of time compared with the classics of Dahl and Tolkien?

Sources
The Not Especially Fascinating Life So Far of J.K. Rowling
http://www.okukbooks.com/harry/rowling/htm
'The Magic of Harry Potter' by Mark Nicholls
(*Eastern Daily Press* 5 July 2000)
'Conjuring up Harry Potter' by Lesley Dobson
(*Sainsbury's Magazine* July 2000)

J.K. Rowling: a biography

J.K. Rowling's first Harry Potter novel was published in 1997. Since then her stories about the young apprentice wizard have sold millions of copies worldwide, making her a famous name in the book world.

Joanne Kathleen Rowling, the elder of two daughters, was born in Gloucestershire in 1965. Her first memory of story-telling was as a child of six when she created tales for her younger sister Di – many of which featured rabbits. "We badly wanted a rabbit," she remembers.

Later, at school, she continued to develop her skills when entertaining friends during lunch breaks with long serial stories in which they performed heroic and daring deeds.

After studying French and Classics at university, she worked for five years as a secretary. "All I ever liked about working in offices was being able to type up stories on the computer when no one was looking," she recalls. It was on a train journey to London at this time that the idea for Harry Potter first came to her.

Note: this section contains facsimiles of OHTs/posters which do not also appear as copymasters.

10

Newspaper report on J.K. Rowling

Famous writer J.K. Rowling has always been rather a wizard at storytelling. Even from an early age she would entertain younger sister Di with her imaginative stories. With this creative gift, she would conjure up a world of her own and enjoy experiences missing in her real world.

From *The Not Especially Fascinating Life So Far of J.K. Rowling* © www.okukbooks.com

---

9

You'll never believe what Joe has been doing now. He calmly announced last week that he was going to try to overcome his fear of being in small spaces – he hates lifts as you know. So he joined a group of pot-holers and spent last weekend crawling through miles of dark and narrow tunnels. He was really worried at first, he says, but he felt so much part of the team that he forgot his fears. How about that! He was even able to help a poor soul who became stuck!

Joe is a conscientious and enthusiastic worker and he is very keen to learn new skills. He thinks deeply about many subjects and always tries to develop his knowledge and understanding of the world.

He has the ability to do well in most subjects but shows a particular flair for design.

Although he has a lot to offer, he seems unsure of himself when presenting his ideas or work to large groups, preferring to be a listener.

Joe is always very thoughtful and well-mannered and he shows a caring attitude towards others.

We have found Joe to be a keen worker, always willing to develop his skills and willing to learn from the experience of others. He is very organised in his approach to jobs and can be relied upon to complete them to a high standard. His designs are well thought through and exhibit a natural flair.

He has proved to be a very useful and reliable member of the team in many ways, playing his part to the full.

He has a caring personality and a polite nature which has made him popular with both staff and clients.

10

Note: this section contains facsimiles of OHTs/posters which do not also appear as copymasters.

12

Mystery story with flashbacks

Fishing for Clues (extract 1)

Almost afraid to breathe, Candy opened Benjamin's diary. It was simply a fat school exercise book, but Benjamin had logged something down faithfully every day from January 1st to June 22nd of the previous year …

"What does it say? Go on, read it," Jake urged, hanging over her shoulder.

Candy hesitated. It didn't seem right – reading someone's private thoughts. "Oh, I don't know …"

"You've got to. It might be important," Jake pestered … Guiltily she looked down at the flamboyant handwriting. "Read it aloud, Candy," Jake begged …

> June 19th, 7p.m. It was all over the newspapers! Well, who'd have believed it! Now this will ruffle a few feathers. Could earn me a pound or two if I just let slip that I know all about it …

Candy stared at her brother. "Jake, I think Benjamin Fisher was a bit of a blackmailer …"

Jake's eyes widened. "You don't think that someone got fed up with him blackmailing them, and got rid of him, do you?"

Candy bit her lip. "I think that's quite likely."

Jake inched closer. "Keep reading."

From *Fishing for Clues* by Ann Evans

© Cambridge University Press 2001

11

Mystery story with flashbacks

Fishing for Clues (plot synopsis)

The story starts with the discovery of the body of Benjamin Fisher, a middle-aged man who used to own a canal boat. He is found in the canal by a girl called Candy. Some people think that he drowned accidentally, but Candy and her brother Jake try to find out how he really died.

They find a box of illegal brandy on his boat, the same brand that is being sold in the local pub by Katherine and Kieran Eastwood. They also find his diary, which includes information about the postwoman. He is blackmailing her because he saw her burn some post instead of delivering it.

The children find out that the lock keeper, Ted Johnstone, is hiding the fact that a boy was killed in his lock many years before. He is about to get an award for fifty years' service, but Benjamin Fisher is threatening to tell the truth.

Candy finds out that the small, nervous fisherman, Arthur Rathbone, is actually a martial arts expert and used to own a jewellery shop. She reads in an old newspaper about a robbery at the jewellery shop the previous year, and then finds Arthur Rathbone fishing in the canal with a magnet.

Finally, the children find a kettle painting by Benjamin Fisher, which shows Arthur Rathbone fishing and catching a box of jewels. This final piece of evidence proves that Arthur Rathbone killed Benjamin Fisher. Benjamin knew that Arthur had robbed his own shop and hidden the jewels in the canal. He had threatened to go to the police unless Arthur paid him money, so Arthur killed him.

Based on *Fishing for Clues* by Ann Evans

© Cambridge University Press 2001

Note: this section contains facsimiles of OHTs/posters which do not also appear as copymasters.

15

Mystery story with flashbacks

Fishing for Clues (extract 2)

"If we're going to bump into a dead body on this boat," Candy Everton announced, following her dad and younger brother, Jake, along the canal towpath, "I'm not getting on to it!"

"Not again!" her dad groaned. "I keep telling you, no one has died. The original owner simply abandoned the *Baloo*. The canal authorities finally claimed her and they've sold her to me. It's all perfectly legal."

Suddenly there was a commotion ... Candy looked up to find a large narrowboat heading straight for them – at top speed ...

At the last second, the speeding craft veered slightly and Mr Everton managed to push it further away with the bargepole so that it only grazed them. But ... the wake from the other narrowboat had churned and dredged up the sludge from the depths ...

Candy stared in disgust at the pile of old clothing tangled in ropes that surfaced and floated alongside the *Baloo*.

"Honestly, the things people throw into canals ..." Her voice faded away. The pile of old clothing was taking on a distinct form. Trousers, a shirt – its arms outstretched. Gloves – grey-white gloves. Only they weren't gloves – they were hands.

And then a face. A face which bobbed up and out of the black, swirling depths. Not much of a face, but a face none the less. With a black beard. With hair. But a sightless face that was long, long dead.

"Dad ..." Candy croaked, knowing she would have to find a louder voice if she wanted to make him hear. "Dad," she tried again. "Dad, I think I know what happened to Benjamin Fisher ..."

From *Fishing for Clues* by Ann Evans

© Cambridge University Press 2001

13

Mystery story with flashbacks

Step by Wicked Step

Even before they reached the haunted house, the night had turned wild. The face of the minibus driver flickered from blue to white under the lightning. Each peal of thunder made the map in Mr Plumley's hand shiver. And the five leftover pupils from Stagfire School peered anxiously through the rain-spattered windows into the storm and the black night.

"There!"

"Where?"

"Over there. See? Up that overgrown driveway."

As the driver swung the minibus into the looming hole between the wrought-iron gates, the three on the right-hand side of the bus read out the words on the peeling sign.

"Old Harwick Hall ..."

*****

The five of them trailed up the vast staircase after Mr Plumley. Each livid flash of lightning through the stained glass above their heads lit their way further up, and further on, through the huge, echoing mansion. Fronds of strange plants stretched from their pots and fingered them as they passed. Disturbed ornaments chattered on mahogany sideboards. And grim Harwicks of all ages stared down at them through hardened, oil-painted eyes.

"Let's try up here."

OLD HARWICK HALL

© Cambridge University Press 2001

From *Step by Wicked Step* by Anne Fine (extracts from pages 1 and 4)

Note: this section contains facsimiles of OHTs/posters which do not also appear as copymasters.

Balanced report

WHALING –
TRADITION OR TRAGEDY? (extract 1)

In 1986 the International Whaling Commission banned commercial whaling. There is now a dispute between whaling countries and anti-whaling countries (two of the most prominent countries involved being Japan and the USA). Whaling countries argue that it is possible to hunt some species of whale commercially without them becoming extinct. Anti-whaling countries argue that all whales are endangered and therefore hunting any species will lead to their extinction.

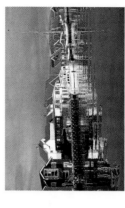

Some communitites in Norway depend on whaling

Pro-whalers believe that the Minke species in particular would not be endangered by hunting, as there are 900,000 Minke whales in the world's oceans and that number is rising. Although anti-whalers recognise this, they believe that the number is still relatively low and commercial hunting of Minke whales would ultimately lead to their extinction.

© Cambridge University Press 2001

Mystery story with flashbacks

The Charge of the Light Brigade

Half a league, half a league,
Half a league onward,
All in the valley of Death
Rode the six hundred.
"Forward, the Light Brigade!
Charge for the guns!" he said:
Into the valley of Death
Rode the six hundred.

Cannon to right of them,
Cannon to left of them,
Cannon in front of them
Volley'd and thunder'd;
Storm'd at with shot and shell,
Boldly they rode and well,
Into the jaws of Death,
Into the mouth of Hell
Rode the six hundred.

The Charge of the Mouse Brigade

Half an inch, half an inch,
Half an inch onward,
Into Cat Valley
Rode the Six Hundred.
"Forward the Mouse Brigade!
Ravage their fleas!" he said.
"Capture the cheese!" he said.

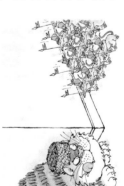

From 'The Charge of the Light Brigade' by Alfred, Lord Tennyson and 'The Charge of the Mouse Brigade' by Bernard Stone

© Cambridge University Press 2001

Note: this section contains facsimiles of OHTs/posters which do not also appear as copymasters.

19

Point

1 Homework improves the relationship between parents and children.
2 Children do not perform better at school as a result of doing homework.
3 Pupils should spend some of their spare time on homework.
4 Homework causes arguments between parents and children.
5 Children who do homework get better exam results.
6 Children should not be doing extra schoolwork at home. All work should be done in school.

Evidence

1 Children are tired at the end of a school day and need to spend their spare time doing other activities such as sport and music and having time to play.
2 Parents are interested in what their children are learning about in school and they spend time together talking, rather than watching television.
3 Research carried out by OFSTED shows that children who regularly complete their homework get better exam results.
4 Children only spend 13% of their time in school. Therefore, a reasonable amount of homework each night helps their education and also allows time for them to take part in other activities.
5 Parents force children to do their homework.
6 Research carried out by Durham University shows that children who do more than ten minutes of homework every night do not score higher on tests.

18

WHALING –
TRADITION OR TRAGEDY? (extract 2)

Whales have been hunted for thousands of years and some communities depend upon the industry for their livelihood. Whaling is an important part of the tradition and culture of nations such as Japan and Norway. While anti-whaling countries acknowledge this, they believe that it is wrong to kill intelligent, endangered animals and that traditional whaling communities could catch other types of fish in order to support themselves.

A further point of dispute is whether new killing methods using explosive harpoons are humane. Whaling nations assert that the whale dies instantly but some scientists dispute this. They argue that only 30% of Minke whales killed by explosives do die immediately. According to a biologist with Eurogroup Animal Welfare, some whales have been paralysed by these weapons and were then pulled onto boats and 'butchered' while still alive.

The strongest argument put forward in favour of commercial whaling is that there are now large numbers of some whale species in the ocean. As numbers of Minke whales rise, it is perhaps difficult to see the justification in protecting this particular species. However, those against whaling argue just as strongly that the numbers of all whale species are still too low and that, consequently, some species will become extinct if any commercial whaling is allowed. What is certain is that if whaling is to continue then the question of humane killing methods needs to be addressed.

Note: this section contains facsimiles of OHTs/posters which do not also appear as copymasters.

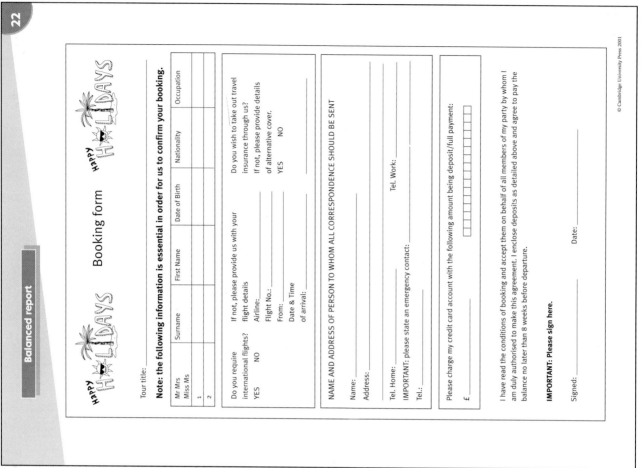

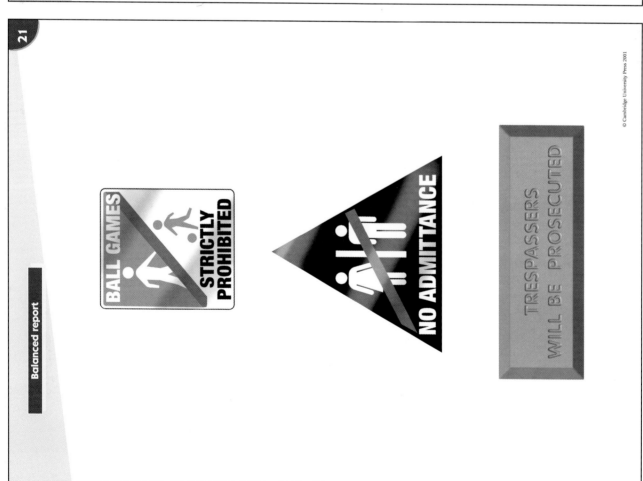

Note: this section contains facsimiles of OHTs/posters which do not also appear as copymasters.

Book review

Harry Potter and the Philosopher's Stone

The author takes Harry from his disastrous first Halloween, through his miserable years with the Dursleys, and up to the age of about eleven when he finishes his first magic year at Hogwarts. The main theme is about good and evil and the clever plot, full of twists and turns, tells how Harry meets Voldemort, the dark sorcerer who killed his parents. Although the suspense is carefully built, there is one problem – nobody could possibly believe that such an interesting character would really be 'written-off' in his first book. Clearly, J.K. Rowling is going to write a series of books about her wonderful wizarding world.

As well as lots of interesting and exciting 'normal' words, the story contains a delightful, fun-filled glossary of made-up names for characters and places. Perhaps best of all, Harry turns out to be a premier league player in a game called Quidditch, which is played with a Quaffle, two Bludgers and a Golden Snitch! Along with all the spells, charms and potions, it is a recipe for excitement and enjoyment.

This book is good for older children and young teenagers – maybe even for fun-loving adults too! Obviously, anyone who likes stories containing magic and imagination will like this book. Also, readers who enjoy adventures or mysteries should appreciate the action and the suspense. Some readers may find the style old-fashioned, but most will enjoy a great story, well told.

Book review

Harry Potter and the Philosopher's Stone

HARRY POTTER AND THE PHILOSOPHER'S STONE
by J.K. Rowling
Published by Bloomsbury Publishing Plc, 1997

HARRY POTTER IS FAST BECOMING THE MOST FAMOUS BOY IN THE WORLD!

This is a magical tale about how a hand-me-down orphan grows into a whizzing wizard! When he is just a baby, Harry Potter's parents – a witch and a wizard – die protecting him from The Dark Side. He is brought up by his normal 'Muggle' relatives, the Dursleys, who treat him very badly. On his tenth birthday he is summoned to Hogwarts School of Witchcraft and Wizardry to meet his destiny. The author keeps it all (almost) believable by making Harry seem a lot like a normal boy, despite his magic powers and his amazing adventures.

The Dursleys are absolutely awful – just too hard to believe in. However, this makes them even more of a contrast with Harry. When Harry makes lots of great magic friends at Hogwarts, the Dursleys become just a background nuisance. His best friends are Ron and Hermione. J.K. Rowling makes sure they're great fun, and always up to crazy tricks. The teachers at Hogwarts are weird and wonderful! The story keeps us on the edge of our seats when one of them turns out to be in league with the forces of evil!

Most of the story happens at Hogwarts School. Here, the author has created fascinating details, like dormitories with guardian ghosts and a Hall with a real starry sky in the ceiling. There are dungeons and secret passages galore! Around every corner and behind every locked door can be found trolls, spectres, dragons, unicorns … to name just a few!

Note: this section contains facsimiles of OHTs/posters which do not also appear as copymasters.

© Cambridge University Press 2001

Book review

Harry Potter and the Philosopher's Stone

Harry had never even imagined such a strange and splendid place. It was lit by thousands and thousands of candles which were floating in mid-air over four long tables, where the rest of the students were sitting. These tables were laid with glittering golden plates and goblets. At the top of the Hall was another long table where the teachers were sitting. Professor McGonagall led the first-years up here, so that they came to a halt in a line facing the other students, with the teachers behind them. The hundreds of faces staring at them looked like pale lanterns in the flickering candlelight. Dotted here and there among the students, the ghosts shone misty silver. Mainly to avoid all the staring eyes, Harry looked upwards, and saw a velvety black ceiling dotted with stars. He heard Hermione whisper, "It's bewitched to look like the sky outside, I read about it in *Hogwarts, a History*."

From Harry Potter and the Philosopher's Stone by J.K. Rowling

---

© Cambridge University Press 2001

Book review

The Great Elephant Chase

"I'm not going to wait around here and let Mr Jackson steal my elephant."
"You're going to *take* Kush?"
"That's right. And you're going to help me!"

Penniless and parentless, Tad and Cissie are on the run from the tyrannical Mr Jackson. Despite the challenge of rivers, prairies and their assorted inhabitants, Tad is spurred on by Cissie's faith in a proper home waiting for them across America. But hiding an enormous elephant is no easy task, and Tad realizes that he must find courage and determination if they are ever to reach their destination.

"A wonderful tale of children and a performing elephant."
Daily Express

"This is writing at its best."
School Librarian

Note: this section contains facsimiles of OHTs/posters which do not also appear as copymasters.

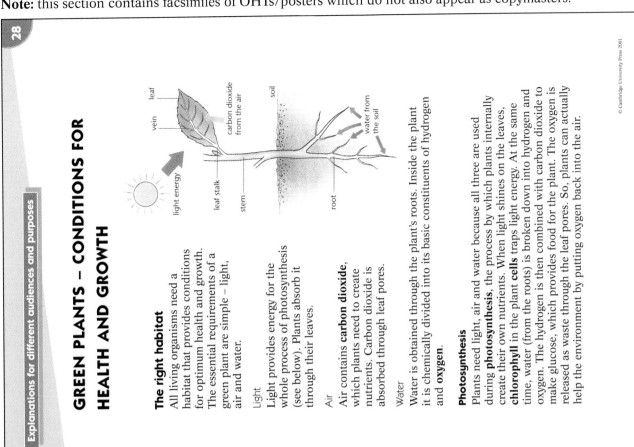

28

Explanations for different audiences and purposes

GREEN PLANTS – CONDITIONS FOR HEALTH AND GROWTH

Diagram labels: light energy; leaf; vein; leaf stalk; stem; carbon dioxide from the air; soil; water from the soil; root

The right habitat

All living organisms need a habitat that provides conditions for optimum health and growth. The essential requirements of a green plant are simple – light, air and water.

Light

Light provides energy for the whole process of photosynthesis (see below). Plants absorb it through their leaves.

Air

Air contains **carbon dioxide**, which plants need to create nutrients. Carbon dioxide is absorbed through leaf pores.

Water

Water is obtained through the plant's roots. Inside the plant it is chemically divided into its basic constituents of hydrogen and **oxygen**.

Photosynthesis

Plants need light, air and water because all three are used during **photosynthesis**, the process by which plants internally create their own nutrients. When light shines on the leaves, **chlorophyll** in the plant **cells** traps light energy. At the same time, water (from the roots) is broken down into hydrogen and oxygen. The hydrogen is then combined with carbon dioxide to make glucose, which provides food for the plant. The oxygen is released as waste through the leaf pores. So, plants can actually help the environment by putting oxygen back into the air.

27

Book review

Haiku

Purple flowers climb
reaching greedily skyward
a promise of rain.

Hills lost in the mist
a spring watercolour forms
rain drops, nature's brush.

Full moon with halo
shining cool benevolence
brings false hope of rain.

Gently pattering
rain, dropping from rose petals
soft, a mother's tears.

Haiku by Adam Roberts

Note: this section contains facsimiles of OHTs/posters which do not also appear as copymasters.

Caring for your houseplant

Congratulations! You are now the proud owner of a foliage houseplant ideal for starting an indoor garden. Leafy plants have only three basic needs – water, light and air. They will stay green and healthy for many years if you care for them correctly. Here are some basic tips about plant care and nutrition:

1 Water your plant regularly and keep the soil damp. This is because plants take in water through their roots. Special cells in the leaves break the water down into hydrogen and oxygen. The plant helps the environment by putting the oxygen back into the air! The hydrogen, however, is needed for photosynthesis – a process by which plants actually create their own food!

2 Place the plant in a sunny position where it will get lots of light.

3 Turn the plant frequently.

4 Keep the plant free of dust.

5 Make sure the plant is in a well-aired place.

WARNING: If foliage plants are deprived of water, light or air for even a short time, they cannot make nutrients. Health damage will quickly occur. Green leaves turn an unhealthy yellow, then stems and leaves wilt and droop. The plant may recover from a temporary problem, but a long time without light, air or water could kill it.

© Cambridge University Press 2001

What happens when the habitat is unsuitable

However, if a plant is deprived of light, air or water, it cannot photosynthesise and make glucose. The plant is affected as follows:

• Green cells deteriorate to yellow.
• Leaves and stems wilt.
• Roots dehydrate and shrivel.

If conditions improve the plant may recover, but it will die if it suffers prolonged deprivation.

Glossary

carbon dioxide	A gas that is made from the elements carbon and oxygen.
cells (living)	The building blocks that plants and animals are made from.
chlorophyll	A pigment found in plant cells which colours them green.
oxygen	One of the two main gases in the air.

© Cambridge University Press 2001

Note: this section contains facsimiles of OHTs/posters which do not also appear as copymasters.

32

4th November 1929

This penicillium stuff is fantastic! It's growing like a weed! I grow it in my laboratory in a sort of rich liquid called a nutrient broth. I pour the broth into small petri dishes, then add some mould spores. It's a pretty messy job, but we scientists have to suffer for our work! I put the dishes in an incubator and let my magic micro-organism grow in the warmth. At the same time I grow some nasty bacteria – in different dishes of course! When I put the penicillium mould in with the bacteria, it has fantastic results. Very quickly you can see that the bacteria nearest the mould stop growing and multiplying. In fact they die off! I think this new antibiotic could be the cure for tonsillitis, pneumonia and many other diseases.

31

Extract 1

The right habitat

All living organisms need a habitat that provides conditions for optimum health and growth. The essential requirements of a green plant are simple – light, air and water.

Extract 2

Leafy plants have only three basic needs – water, light and air. They will stay green and healthy for many years if you care for them correctly. Here are some basic tips about plant care and nutrition.

Extract 3

Photosynthesis

Plants need light, air and water because all three are used during photosynthesis, the process by which plants internally create their own nutrients. When light shines on the leaves, **chlorophyll** in the plant **cells** traps light energy. At the same time, water (from the roots) is broken down into hydrogen and oxygen. The hydrogen is then combined with carbon dioxide to make glucose, which provides food for the plant. The oxygen is released as waste through the leaf pores. So, plants can actually help the environment by putting oxygen back into the air.

Extract 4

Water your plant regularly and keep the soil damp. This is because plants take in water through their roots. Special cells in the leaves break the water down into hydrogen and oxygen. The plant helps the environment by putting the oxygen back into the air! The hydrogen, however, is needed for photosynthesis – a process by which plants actually create their own food!

Term one fiction focus:
1 How to write in the style of a classic story

What most children will already know:

How stories are structured to a pattern of build-up/sequence/complication/resolution

That the author and narrator of the story are not necessarily the same

How the viewpoint of the narrator affects the narrative

What children will learn in this unit:

How to write in the voice and style of a classic text

How to plan narrative writing quickly and effectively

How to summarise text

 1 **Classic story style**

Objectives

To analyse key linguistic and stylistic features
To write in the voice and style of a classic text

Shared session

You need: OHT/poster 1, paper for masking text, large sheet of paper for class poster, coloured pens.

*This unit is based on Robert Louis Stevenson's **Treasure Island**. The material will be accessible to children whether or not they have read the book, but it is recommended that they are encouraged to read the story or that it is read aloud as a class text.*

■ Display and read the first two sentences from OHT/poster 1, masking the rest of the text.

■ Ask children to identify any unusual words and phrases, and discuss their meaning in this context (e.g. *lighted brand, capture was thus assured, log-house*). What do they think has happened?

■ Ask children if they think the sentence is taken from a fiction or non-fiction text. Do they think it is written by a contemporary writer? Why/why not?

■ Tell them to look for further clues as they listen to the rest of the extract, and if possible, to identify the text it comes from. Display and read the rest of OHT/poster 1.

■ Discuss what children know about the story of *Treasure Island* and its author, R.L. Stevenson. If necessary, explain that it was written in 1883, but is set in the 1700s. It is about Jim Hawkins, a cabin boy on board the ship *Hispaniola*, which is searching for gold hidden by pirates. When they reach Treasure Island the crew, led by the ship's cook Long John Silver, mutiny and go off to try to find the treasure for themselves. They take possession of a log cabin and are sleeping there when Jim disturbs them, thinking that his friends, the Captain and the Doctor, are hiding there. OHT/poster 1 describes what happens next.

■ Ask children for clues in the text that show how Jim feels when he is captured. Underline these and discuss what they reveal about Jim (e.g. that he is afraid – *the worst of my apprehensions realised*; brave – *pluckily enough, I hope*; despairing – *with black despair in my heart*). Discuss how the **first person narrative** means we see things through Jim's eyes.

■ Tell children that over the next few sessions they are going to be writing more of Jim's story in the style of R.L. Stevenson. First they are going to look in more detail at the language he uses. Discuss vocabulary that will <u>not</u> be used, for example modern slang. Ask what Jim would mean if he described something as 'wicked'.

- ■ With the children, identify and underline other examples of words and phrases that show this story is not contemporary (e.g. *fine broadcloth suit, a loan of the link, stick the glim in the wood heap*). Ensure that children understand the meaning of these words.

- ■ Point out that many of the phrases used sound very formal to a modern reader and ask for some examples (e.g. *… in which he had fulfilled his mission, And thereupon he sat down, … as may be well supposed*).

- ■ Read some of the dialogue and discuss its purpose (e.g. to reveal character, move narrative on, create tension). What does the dialogue show us about the character of the pirates?

- ■ Explain that the last sentence is typical of Stevenson's style. Ask children what they notice about its structure and punctuation (long and complex, with several subordinate clauses divided by a semi-colon and commas). Ask about the effect of this sentence (it gives a detailed insight into Jim's state of mind; it creates suspense).

- ■ Discuss the effects of other sentence structures (e.g. long descriptive passages slow the narrative down and create atmosphere, short sentences can speed up the pace and make the text more exciting).

Group follow-up activities

1 red   pupil's book page 4

Children read a passage from *Treasure Island*, identifying an expression which shows that this is not a modern story. With a partner, they discuss things that Jim might see/hear/smell when he goes ashore.

Guided group support   Focus on the powerful adjectives used (*stagnant, sodden, rotting*). Help children to think of adjectives they can use to give the reader a clear picture of the things they imagine on the island.

2 blue/yellow   pupil's book page 5   (copymaster 1)

Children read a passage from *Treasure Island*, identifying expressions which show that this is not a modern story. With a partner, they discuss things that Jim might see/hear/smell when he goes ashore, and which adjectives could be used to describe them.

Guided group support   Encourage discussion and debate. Look closely at unusual words and phrases and encourage the children to make sensible guesses about meanings.

3 blue/yellow   pupil's book page 6

If time, children complete a sentence that follows on from the passage they have just read. They should write in the style of R.L. Stevenson. A list of archaic vocabulary is provided to help them.

Plenary   Recap significant points about the style of *Treasure Island* (e.g. the differences in language used by the pirates and other characters, the formal, old-fashioned vocabulary signalling the age of the text, the complex sentence structure and punctuation). Make a class poster entitled 'How to write in the style of a classic story' and write up notes on the key language features you have just discussed. If any children completed activity 3, read out some of their sentences as well as the real next sentence from the text: *Then I came to a long thicket of these oak-like trees – live, or evergreen oaks, I heard afterwards they should be called – which grew low along the sand like brambles, the boughs curiously twisted, the foliage compact, like thatch.* Challenge the children to guess which was written by R.L. Stevenson. Ask how they could tell which was the real author's sentence.

2 Narrative viewpoint

Objectives   To manipulate narrative perspective by writing in the voice and style of a classic text

To manipulate narrative perspective by writing with two different narrators

Shared session   *You need: OHT/poster 1, 'How to write in the style of a classic story' poster (from Session 1), large sheet of paper, coloured pens.*

■   Recap the **narrative viewpoint** in *Treasure Island*. What effect does this have on the reader? (The reader sympathises with Jim because they see things through his eyes.)

■   Recap the scene children read in Session 1. Discuss what impression Stevenson wanted to give about:
  ○   the situation Jim found himself in;
  ○   the different characters in the scene.

■   Ask children how they feel about the characters. What do they hope happens to them next? Why?

■   Would they think the same thing if there was a different narrator, for example Long John Silver? Tell them to imagine the scene through Long John Silver's eyes as they listen to the extract. Display and re-read OHT/poster 1.

■   Discuss children's ideas (e.g. Silver might feel surprised to see Jim. He might think he is spying on him and his men and feel angry).

■   Point out that the **style** as well as the viewpoint would be different if Silver were narrating. With the children, identify and underline aspects of the style Stevenson uses for Long John Silver:
  ○   'piratespeak' vocabulary (e.g. *shiver my timbers, bring yourselves to, you may lay to that*). Discuss possible origins of these nautical expressions.
  ○   unconventional grammar (e.g. *this here gets away from me clean, it do*). What effect is created by Silver's style of speech? What does the author want us to think about Silver's background and education?

■   Compare Jim's choice of words with Silver's speech (e.g. his sentences are generally longer and more complex, his grammar is more conventional and his vocabulary is more formal).

■   With the children, rewrite the first few sentence of this extract with Silver as narrator. Describe Jim through Silver's eyes and try to include some dialogue, for example:

>   I were fair amazed when I see we'd a-captured young Jim. He stood there, afore us, all pale and shiverin'.
>   "Mr Silver," says he, "I desire to know what it is you intend to do with me."

■   Put in some vocabulary that emulates Stevenson's and creates a sense of the period in which the story was written. For example, choose 'beheld' instead of 'saw', 'addressed' instead of 'spoke'.

■   Tell children that they are now going to carry on writing with Long John Silver as narrator.

Group follow-up activities

1 red   **pupil's book page 7**

Children write about what happens after Jim has been captured, using Long John Silver as the narrator. Some ideas and a word bank containing helpful words and phrases are provided.

Guided group support   Encourage children to include a conversation between Jim and Silver, ensuring that they make the two characters speak in obviously different ways. Give examples of words and phrases they can use.

2 blue/yellow   **pupil's book page 8**

Children write about what happens after Jim has been captured, first using Jim as the narrator, and then writing a second version with Long John Silver narrating. Some ideas and a word bank containing helpful words and phrases are provided.

Guided group support   Help children choose words and phrases that emulate Jim's narrative voice. Discuss changes that need to be made if Silver is the narrator.

Plenary   Ask for volunteers to read out their writing to the class. Discuss how the viewpoint changes, as well as the style of the writing, when the narrator is changed. Ask children to suggest more vocabulary to add to the 'How to write in the style of a classic story' poster (especially 'piratespeak' words).

3 Planning the story

Objective   To plan effectively the plot, characters and structure of narrative writing

Shared session   *You need: a large sheet of paper and coloured pens.*

- Tell children that you are going to plan and write a class story based on *Treasure Island*.

- Identify the target audience (e.g. plan to read the stories to another class, display them in a public area or present them in an assembly).

- Elicit the key elements of story structure and the order in which they appear (beginning, middle, end). Use this to draw up a planning framework on a large sheet of paper. Remember to include: beginning – setting, characters, problem; middle – events, build-up and climax; ending – resolution).

- Decide on a basic plot for the class story, and write this on the framework under a separate heading (e.g. Jim has escaped from the pirates and found the treasure. He is returning to the *Hispaniola* with Long John Silver as a prisoner when Silver escapes).

- Plan the rest of the story on the framework. Make notes on:
  - the **setting**. What condition is the ship in? How does it look inside? Is there much food left?
  - the **characters**. Are any other characters involved apart from Jim and Silver?
  - the **problem**. How does Silver escape?
  - the **events** and **build-up to the climax**. How does Jim go about finding Silver? Does he work alone or get help?
  - the **resolution**. Does Jim manage to recapture Silver or not?

■ Remind children that adding further events will make the story more interesting but also more complex. It is important that the events are linked and that the ending resolves the problem.

■ Ask children to suggest titles for the class story. Choose one, and write it up.

■ Tell children that they are now going to plan their own stories based on *Treasure Island*.

Group follow-up activities

1 red   pupil's book page 9   copymaster 2

Children plan their own stories using the ideas suggested or their own alternatives. They use the copymaster to plan their story.

Guided group support Encourage children to make their planning notes brief but clear.

2 blue/yellow   pupil's book page 9

Children plan their own stories using the ideas suggested or their own alternatives. They draw up a plan for their story by themselves.

Guided group support

Blue Encourage children to include more than one problem and related event.

Yellow Challenge children to show you how the problems and events link together.

Plenary

Discuss any problems with the planning frameworks. Ensure that all the children have completed their plans and ask for volunteers to share their plans and to explain what they have done.

---

4 Drafting the story

Objective

To write a first draft using the plan

Shared session

You need: class story plan, 'How to write in the style of a classic story' poster (from Session 1), large sheet of paper, coloured pens.

See **Drafting** on page 7 for more detailed advice on conducting a whole-class drafting session.

■ Tell children you are now going to draft your class story based on *Treasure Island*, using the plan made in the previous session. Explain that you will use your 'How to write in the style of a classic story' poster for help.

■ Elicit that the beginning of the story has to set the scene and draw the reader into the story so that they want to continue reading. Encourage children to suggest words to do with sight, smell and sound to create a vivid picture of the scene.

■ Recap the differences in Jim and Silver's ways of speaking and model these in your writing.

■ Ensure that you model other linguistic features of classic texts (e.g. complex sentences with lots of subordinate clauses, formal phrases, etc.). Use the 'How to write in the style of a classic story' poster for reference throughout.

■ Listen to and act upon children's suggestions and incorporate them into the draft. Point out that it is helpful to read back over what you have written to help you check the progress of your writing.

- Remind children that this is only a first draft, and they will have a chance to improve the text in the next session.
- Ask children to identify the features which make the writing like the style of R.L. Stevenson.
- Tell children that they are now going to draft their own stories based on *Treasure Island*.

Group follow-up activities

red/blue/yellow

Children draft their own stories, using their plans from Session 3.

Guided group support

Red Encourage speed. Do not allow children to use dictionaries or thesauruses at this stage (they will use them in the next session).

Blue/Yellow Remind children to use their knowledge of the text to help them emulate the author's style. Refer to the 'How to write in the style of a classic story' poster and the word banks on pages 6–7 of the pupil's book.

Plenary

Ask volunteers to read out their work. Make constructive but positive comments and encourage children to do the same. Discuss any difficulties which arose during the drafting process.

---

⑤ Revising and editing the story

Objective

To edit the story draft with particular reference to style and linguistic features

Shared session

You need: class story draft, thesaurus, coloured pen (different colour from those used in Session 4).

*See **Revising and editing** on page 7 for more detailed advice.*

- Tell children that you are going to look at ways of improving your class story.
- Choose some or all of the following revising and editing focuses for your redrafting session:
  - presentation of dialogue;
  - use of punctuation;
  - paragraphing;
  - spelling;
  - vocabulary: is it varied and appropriate to the period?
- Read through your first draft, asking children to suggest improvements according to the chosen focus. Write these on the draft using a different colour.
- If necessary, use a thesaurus to find more varied vocabulary and to avoid repetition.
- Tell children that they are now going to revise and edit their own stories.

Group follow-up activities

red/blue/yellow

Assign a redrafting focus to each of the children before they start editing their texts. Write this at the top of their sheets.

Children revise and edit their stories. Get children to work in pairs, explaining to each other what changes they are going to make to their text.

Guided group support

Red Help children to use a dictionary and thesaurus to check and improve their texts.

Blue/Yellow Check that the vocabulary is appropriate and discuss words that need to be changed. Suggest alternatives if necessary. Help children to improve sentence structure as well as vocabulary.

Plenary Ask for volunteers to share their revised stories, giving examples of things they changed. Ask the class to comment constructively on the changes made.

6 Publishing the story

Objective To bring the writing to a standard suitable for presentation

Shared session *You need: revised class story draft, examples of classic story books, large sheet of paper, coloured pens.*

 *See **Publishing** on page 8 for more detailed notes on the issues involved in the final presentation of the text.*

- Tell children that you are now ready to publish your class story.

- Recap on your chosen target audience and their needs. Make sure children understand that the main aim is to lay the story out clearly and attractively, adding illustrations which contribute to the enjoyment of the text without being too distracting.

- Display some examples of classic story books. Look at how the text is laid out, how the chapters are divided, and whether any illustration is used. What style of illustration do children think is most appropriate for the class story?

- Discuss features of effective presentation. For example:
  - clear handwriting/effective fonts (if using ICT);
  - good spelling;
  - clear layout.

- Discuss possible innovative formats which you could use to 'publish' the stories (e.g. on illustrated sheets folded up like treasure maps). Encourage children to use ICT if practicable.

- Tell children that they are now going to publish their own stories.

Group follow-up activities **red/blue/yellow**

Children work on the final published copies of their own stories.

Guided group support

Red Encourage children to make final checks on spelling and punctuation.

Blue Ask children about their plans for publication. Discuss possibilities for spacing and illustrations.

Yellow Discuss in depth how the intended audience may affect the way in which the story is published.

Plenary Ask for volunteers to display their published stories. Encourage the class to give constructive comments on how the texts are presented. If appropriate, work on presenting the stories to the target audience (e.g. making a wall display, combining the stories into a class book to lend to other classes). Take an overall look at what children have learnt and assess how well the published stories meet the criteria of classic story style.

ADDITIONAL SESSIONS

Writing a modern retelling of a classic story

Objective To manipulate the narrative perspective of a classic story by producing a modern retelling

Shared session *You need: OHT/poster 3, large sheet of paper, coloured pens.*

■ Tell children they are going to read an extract from the beginning of *Treasure Island*. Explain that the captain of the *Hispaniola*, Billy Bones, is renting a room in the Admiral Benbow inn, which is owned by Jim Hawkins' parents. One day, Billy is visited by a former shipmate, Black Dog. The extract describes the first few moments of their meeting. Display and read OHT/poster 3.

■ Explain that you are going to rewrite this text using modern language.

■ Decide how to update the characters and circumstances (e.g. instead of pirates, the captain and Black Dog could be burglars or bank robbers, and the Admiral Benbow could be a pub or hotel).

■ Ask children to identify words that are specific to the period and think of modern alternatives (e.g. *fronted us* – faced us; *returned* – replied; *seen a sight of times* – experienced many things).

■ Recap what children have learnt about R.L. Stevenson's style. Discuss his sentence construction and use of long, densely punctuated sentences. Look at the phrase *he had the look of a man who sees a ghost*. Ask children how they think a modern writer would write this ('he looked as if he had seen a ghost'). Point out that the first paragraph is a single sentence. Ask children how many sentences they think a modern writer would have used to convey this information.

■ Now rewrite the text completely, sentence by sentence. Ask children to suggest how each sentence could be translated into more up-to-date language. Experiment with modern expressions and slang. For example, the sentence:

> "Now, look here," said the captain; "you've run me down; here I am; well, then, speak up: what is it?"

could become:

> "OK Dog, you've got me cornered," said the captain, "so why don't you spit it out – what is it?"

■ Tell children that they are now going to practise retelling classic stories in modern language.

Group follow-up activities **1 red pupil's book page 10**

Using up-to-date language, children retell the episode reproduced in the pupil's book, which describe the events following on from the extract on OHT/poster 3.

Guided group support Encourage children to retain the storyline of the passage provided (they are not required to 'translate' it).

2 blue pupil's book page 11

Children read the first two passages on the spread, then retell the second using up-to-date language.

Guided group support Ensure children understand words like *cutlass* and *chine*. Encourage children to discuss modern alternatives to nineteenth-century words and phrases.

3 yellow   **pupil's book page 11**

Children read all three passages on the spread, then retell the third using up-to-date language.

Guided group support Challenge children to produce a line-by-line 'translation' of the original text.

Plenary   Volunteers read out their retellings or 'translations'. Ask them to identify the changes they made and invite the class to comment on how well they have retold the story. Encourage them to assess the choice of up-to-date vocabulary, the sentence structure and the setting/characterisation.

Writing a story as a playscript

Objective   To rewrite a piece of narrative text as a playscript

Shared session   *You need: OHT/poster 4, large sheet of paper, coloured pens.*

*You might find it helpful to show children a section of **Treasure Island** on video prior to this session (if this is possible).*

■ Revise what children know about writing playscripts. Cover the following:
  - a play is divided into scenes;
  - descriptions of settings help set the scene;
  - there is dialogue between characters;
  - each time a new character speaks the dialogue begins on a new line;
  - characters' thoughts may be presented as asides;
  - stage directions provide instructions to actors; they are displayed in brackets and occur between or within lines of dialogue.

■ Explain to children that you are going to read them an extract from the end of *Treasure Island*. Jim and his friends have loaded the treasure in the hold of the *Hispaniola*, and have set sail. The last three mutineers have been left behind on the island and the crew have to decide whether or not to take pity on them and rescue them. Display and read OHT/poster 4.

■ Ask children to help you describe the setting of this scene for a playscript. For example:

> Jim and the crew are on board ship. Crashing waves and the cries of gulls can be heard in the background. Three pirates kneel at the front of the stage, their arms raised.

Point out that the original narrative <u>implies</u> what kind of dialogue might take place but does not actually provide it. Ask children to suggest what the doctor and the pirates might say to each other, and arrange their words into lines of dialogue, writing this up on a large sheet of paper. Ask them to think carefully about how each of the characters might speak (e.g. the pirates would use 'piratespeak'; the doctor would use a more formal, educated style). Here are some example lines (point out that each new character's dialogue begins on a new line):

Pirate 1	Save us, don't leave us here to rot!
Doctor	Come come man! There is food enough for you all in the clearing, but in England a noose awaits you.
Pirate 2	'ave mercy on us, for pity's sake!

■ Model the writing of a stage direction, for example:

(The doctor turns and starts to move away.)

Draw children's attention to the position of the direction and the use of brackets.

■ Continue to work on the dialogue until you have written a short section of script. Add stage directions and asides as suggested by the children.

■ Ask for volunteers to play different parts as they read the script aloud.

■ Tell children they are now going to practise writing their own playscripts based on *Treasure Island*.

Group activities

1 red   pupil's book page 12

Children prepare a playscript based on an extract from *Treasure Island*, using the setting and characters given.

Guided group support Encourage children to think through basic arguments that will form the dialogue before beginning to write. Remind them how to set out dialogue correctly.

2 blue/yellow   pupil's book page 12

Children prepare a playscript based on an extract from *Treasure Island*, choosing their own setting and characters and adding stage directions.

Guided group support

Blue Encourage children to set out dialogue and stage directions correctly. Remind them that stage directions can suggest sound effects as well as telling the actors how to move.

Yellow Talk through possible styles of speech that the villagers might use. What sort of characters do the children want to portray? Discuss the use of stage directions (e.g. '(nervously)') before a line of dialogue.

Plenary   Ask for volunteers to read/perform their scripts for the class.

Summarising

Objectives   To summarise a key passage from a text in a specified number of words

To use this as a blurb for your story

Shared session   *You need: large sheet of paper, coloured pens, stopwatch.*

■ Explain the concept of a **summary** to children (a short description of key events or important points).

■ Challenge children to summarise one of the following:

- a film they have seen recently;
- an event that happened at playtime;
- a conversation they have had with a friend.

- Remind children of some key points to bear in mind when writing a summary (e.g. write in note form, use abbreviations, only select the most important points).

- Tell children they must give an oral summary in no more than sixty seconds. Give them two minutes to prepare, then ask for volunteers to present their summaries. Time each speaker to make sure they don't overrun.

Do not worry if you run over the word limit slightly – it is intended only as a guide.

- Now explain that you are going to summarise an episode in *Treasure Island* (e.g. Jim's capture by Long John Silver) in 100 words or less. First, ask for volunteers to sum up the episode orally, then begin writing the summary.

- Work on the written summary until it contains all of the key points.

- Ask children about the purpose of summaries (to convey the essential information as concisely as possible). Ask where they might find written summaries in real life (e.g. newspaper headlines, on the back of a video or as a blurb for a book). Explain that the purpose of a book blurb is a bit more specific – it has to make the reader want to read the book as well as giving the essential information.

- Tell children they are going to summarise their own *Treasure Island* stories and use these summaries as blurbs.

Group follow-up activities

red

Children write summaries of their own stories to be used as blurbs. Do not set a word limit for this group.

Guided group support Concentrate on the appropriate selection of key events and points.

blue

As for the red group, but set a limit of fifty words.

Guided group support Encourage children to write their summaries, count the words and then rephrase their writing to make it shorter without omitting any key points.

yellow

As for the red group, but set a word limit of thirty words.

Guided group support After summarising their own stories, challenge children to summarise a lengthier piece of text, for example a chapter from *Treasure Island* or a recently read book.

Plenary

Ask for volunteers to share their summaries and encourage the class to offer constructive comments. Discuss any problems encountered – children usually find it difficult to work to a word limit. Discuss strategies for dealing with this, such as making a first draft and then paring it down to the essential points only.

Writing a poem using active verbs and personification

Objectives

To write poems experimenting with active verbs and personification

To produce revised poems for reading aloud individually

Shared session

You need: OHT/poster 5, paper to mask the text, a large sheet of paper and coloured pens.

■ Display OHT/poster 5, with the title covered.

■ Read the poem aloud, then ask children what they think *it* refers to (the playground). Encourage them to look for clues in the text.

■ Uncover the title. Explain that the technique of giving animal or human attributes to inanimate objects is known as **personification**.

■ Point out that active verbs are often used in personification (e.g. *grabbed*, *grasped*, *fight*, *reach out*). The verbs chosen here suggest that the playground is malevolent.

■ Discuss how snow could be personified. Ask what kind of verbs would be appropriate (active verbs). Ask children to suggest suitable verbs (e.g. 'crept', 'danced', 'floated', 'sparkled', 'whispered'). List their suggestions on a large sheet of paper.

■ Build a few lines of poetry around the suggested words. For example:

> Last night Snow crept into my garden
> It looked around with sparkling eyes
> It danced with the trees, whispered to the plants
> And settled down to sleep on the grass.

■ Ask children to suggest other objects for personification (e.g. other types of weather, household equipment). Can they think of suitable active verbs to describe these things?

Group follow-up activities

1 red   pupil's book page 14

Children make a list of active verbs to use in a 'volcano' poem, and then complete the poem using the framework provided.

Guided group support Help children to extend their writing by suggesting other human or animal characteristics that children could use to describe the volcano.

2 blue/yellow   pupil's book page 14

Children choose a subject from the suggestions provided. They then write a poem that personifies the chosen subject.

Guided group support

Blue Encourage children to think of a simple theme to help (e.g. the moon as a ghost, or a river as a scaly serpent).

Yellow Encourage children to read their poems aloud and to focus on rhythm as well as imagery.

3 yellow   pupil's book page 15

If time, children can edit and improve their poems.

4 red/blue/yellow   pupil's book page 15

If time, children read 'Autumn Gale', and look for examples of objects that are personified (e.g. *leaves*, *hedges*, *plastic bag*, *willow*). They also identify the *big bully* (the wind) and look for active verbs (e.g. *hurtling*, *shivering*, *tugging*, *terrorizing*).

Plenary Invite volunteers to read their work aloud. Highlight successful use of active verbs in personification, and ask the class for their comments.

Homework suggestions

- Make a plan for a classic story and swap it with a partner who has also written a plan. Use your partner's plan to write a story in the style of Robert Louis Stevenson. **(After Sessions 1–4)**

- Read all or part of other classic texts and note down words and phrases that show it is not a modern story. **(After Session 1)**

- Research information about real-life smugglers or pirates. Use the information to make a plan for a story about these characters. **(After Session 3)**

- Read *Kidnapped* or *The Black Arrow*, also by Robert Louis Stevenson. **(After Session 6)**

- Choose a scene from a book you have read recently and rewrite it as a playscript. **(After 'Writing a story as a playscript')**

- Write a summary of a book you read recently to use as a blurb. **(After 'Summarising')**

UNIT **1** ## How to write in the style of a classic story

Colour the right number of stars to show how well you did the following things:

0 stars = I didn't do it.
1 star = I gave it a try.
2 stars = I did it quite well.

3 stars = I did it well.
4 stars = I did an excellent job!

I know what is meant by 'style'.	☆	☆	☆	☆
I identified some important features of Robert Louis Stevenson's style.	☆	☆	☆	☆
I found some period vocabulary in Stevenson's writing.	☆	☆	☆	☆
I understood how different narrators give the reader a different viewpoint.	☆	☆	☆	☆
I rewrote a section of *Treasure Island* with a new narrator.	☆	☆	☆	☆
I changed the narrative viewpoint in my reworking of a section of *Treasure Island*.	☆	☆	☆	☆
I made an effective plan for a piece of narrative writing.	☆	☆	☆	☆
I wrote in the style of Robert Louis Stevenson.	☆	☆	☆	☆
I used vocabulary appropriate to the time of Robert Louis Stevenson.	☆	☆	☆	☆

Something I am especially pleased with

Something my audience liked in my writing

Something I'd like to do better next time

Term one non-fiction focus:
2 How to write a biographical recount

What most children will already know:

The basic structure of a recount

The use of connectives to link paragraphs, sentences, clauses

How to locate and use information for research purposes

How to make notes

How to write a simple character description

What children will learn in this unit:

To use recount structure to write a biography (revision)

To extend their understanding of the use of connectives

The use of quotations in factual writing

The use of evaluative comments

To phrase questions appropriately

To plan and research information for a biography

 Recount structure

Objectives
To revise recount structure

To be able to identify information sources

Shared session
You need: OHTs/posters 6 and 7, 3 different colour pens, 2 large sheets of paper.

■ Tell children that over the next two weeks they will be learning how to write a biography. Explain that they are going to be researching the lives of some interesting people in order to write biographical recounts of them.

■ Write 'biography' and underline 'bio'. Ask for, or give, other words that contain the prefix 'bio', and identify their meanings. Focus on the common element of each definition (i.e. living/life). Explain that 'bio' comes from the Greek *bios*, which means 'life'. Discuss the meaning of the word biography. If necessary, repeat this process for 'auto' to identify the meaning of autobiography (*auto* means 'self' in Greek).

■ Tell children that you are going to find out how to organise a biographical recount about a well-known person. Write the name 'J.K. Rowling' and ask children what they know about her.

■ Ask children what they know about the structure of recounts (they start with an orientation, events are described in chronological order and they end with a reorientation). Display and read OHTs/posters 6 and 7. Number the paragraphs 1 to 6. Ask children to identify the orientation, the key events and the reorientation and use three different coloured pens to draw boxes around these sections as shown below.

> **Orientation**
> J.K. Rowling's first Harry Potter novel ...
> ... making her a famous name in the book world.

> **Key events**
> Joanne Kathleen Rowling, the elder of two daughters ...
> ... turned it into a worldwide success.

> **Reorientation**
> J.K. Rowling's ability to hold her readers spellbound …
> … compared with the classics of Dahl and Tolkien?

■ Ask children, in pairs, to find each piece of information given in the orientation. Collect and list their suggestions in the centre column of a large sheet of paper headed 'Information', which you have divided into three columns (see below for example. You will be filling in the 'Question' column in Session 4.).

■ Ask what each point tells us about the subject. Write the answers in the right-hand column, underlining the question word. For example:

Question	Information	What it tells us
	J.K. Rowling, famous name in book world	<u>Who</u> she is
	first Harry Potter novel about apprentice wizard	<u>What</u> she has done
	published 1997	<u>When</u> this happened
	sold millions of copies	<u>Why</u> she's famous
	worldwide	<u>Where</u> this happened

■ Elicit the purpose of the orientation (it gives key facts that will make clear to the reader who the subject is and what is well known about them).

■ Where could the author of this biography have found the information? (e.g. by interviewing the subject, reading other biographies or articles, using the internet). Point out the sources listed at the bottom of OHT/poster 7. Discuss why it is important that information given in biographies is accurate.

Group follow-up activities

1 red   pupil's book page 16

Children read the orientation from a biography of Isambard Kingdom Brunel. They identify the information and present this on a table as in the shared session.

Guided group support Reinforce the structure of orientations by identifying the details given in other biographies.

2 blue   pupil's book page 17

Children plan and write an orientation for a biography about a family member or friend.

Guided group support Help children to identify and discuss the merits of different sources of information. Which could they use if researching the life of family members or friends?

3 yellow   pupil's book page 17

Children investigate the order in which facts are presented in the orientations for three biographies.

Guided group support Reinforce the importance of maintaining factual accuracy when collecting information for a biographical recount by using a variety of sources to collect and compare information.

Plenary Make a poster entitled 'How to write a biographical recount'. Explain to children this poster will help them when they plan and write their own biographies. Ask children what they have learnt today about biographical recounts in general (e.g. there is usually an orientation giving key information to help the reader, key events are described in chronological order and the recount ends with a reorientation). Ask what information usually goes in the orientation section. Write these points up on the poster. What do children think are the most useful or reliable sources of information for a biographer?

② Using connectives

Objectives To develop understanding of the event section of recounts, and the use of chronological connectives to order the events

To understand that paragraphs, sentences and points within a sentence are each joined by connective words or phrases

Shared session *You need: OHTs/posters 6 and 7, large sheet of paper, coloured pens, 'How to write a biographical recount' poster (from Session 1).*

If time, discuss why an author might choose to write about some aspects in more detail than others (e.g. personal interest or relevance to purpose; amount of space available; sources of information available). Also consider what effect this choice may have on the reader's view of the subject (e.g. it could imply that the subject did not wish to discuss this event during an interview or did not think the event was important). Explain that it is important for a biographer to consider the choices they make about what to include in greater or lesser detail, or what to leave out.

■ Display OHTs/posters 6 and 7. Tell children that you are going to look at how the passing of time is shown in between each key event in the subject's life.

■ Ask children what order the events are described in and why (chronological order, as a biography is meant to take us through a subject's life, from birth to the present day).

■ Identify how tense is used in biographies (usually past tense, although the reorientation may be in present or future tense depending on whether or not the subject is still alive).

■ Ask children what jobs connectives do in texts (they link information in chronological order, introduce more information, present opposite points of view). Explain that you are going to look at how time sequencing connectives are used in biographies.

■ Make a three-column chart with the following headings: 'Connectives linking paragraphs', 'Connectives linking sentences', 'Connectives linking clauses'. Ask children to identify and underline words or phrases from the beginning of paragraphs 3, 4 and 5 which connect them with the previous paragraph and show that events happened in chronological order (*Later, After, A few years later*). Write these in the first column. Can children suggest alternative connectives?

■ Explain that connective words and phrases can also be used to link ideas between sentences. Ask children to find an example of this in paragraph 4 or 5, and to explain which events are being linked. Write up the examples in the second column of the chart and ask for alternatives.

■ On the OHT/poster, underline the sentence beginning *Her first memory* in paragraph 2. Point out how the connective *when* links the clauses, and write this example in the third column. Ask children about the effect of the sentence if the connective is omitted (it sounds very stilted).

■ Make sure children understand that all of these connectives can be used in any of the three ways identified.

■ Ask children to think about the flow of the text as you read paragraphs 2–5 of the biography, leaving out the time connectives (para 2: *when*; para 3: *later*; para 4: *After studying French and Classics at university, at this time*; para 5: *A few years later, Whilst there, After two years, after all this, Eventually*). Elicit what the time connectives do and explain how they help the reader (they make links between one event and the next and they improve the flow for the reader).

Group follow-up activities

1 red   pupil's book page 18   copymaster 3

Children read the biography of Brunel. They identify and label the orientation, key events section and reorientation. They then copy a table in the pupil's book, and complete it with connectives to show the passing of time between paragraphs. Finally, they think of an alternative for each connective.

Guided group support Reinforce understanding of the way that time indicating connectives help a piece of writing to flow by reading it without the connectives and discussing the effect.

2 blue   pupil's book page 18   copymaster 4

Children read the biography of Steven Spielberg. They identify and label the orientation, key events section and reorientation. They then copy a table in the pupil's book, and complete it with connectives that link events together within the same paragraph. Finally, they think of an alternative for each connective.

Guided group support As for the red group.

3 yellow   pupil's book page 19   copymaster 4

Children underline any words or phrases that are time connectives. They choose the paragraph with the most time connectives and rewrite it, using alternatives.

Guided group support Help children to use connectives to order events chronologically.

Alternative group activities

blue

Children reinforce understanding of the phrases that help to link ideas within paragraphs by finding examples in other texts and adding them to the 'Connectives' chart from the shared session.

yellow

Children use time connectives in sentences about J.K. Rowling or Spielberg.

Plenary   Ask children to explain what they have learnt about the 'key events' section of a biographical recount (it covers the main aspects of a person's life; the events are in chronologically ordered paragraphs; the paragraphs can be linked by time connectives; time connectives can also link ideas within a paragraph). Write their observations on the 'How to write a biographical recount' poster from Session 1 under the heading 'Key events'.

③ Quotations and evaluative comments

Objectives   To understand that quotations provide information about people's thoughts and feelings, as well as additional personal details

To understand that evaluative comments are based on factual information but are influenced by personal opinion

Shared session   *You need: OHTs/posters 6 and 7, 'How to write a biographical recount' poster (from Session 1), 'Connectives' chart (from Session 2).*

■   Explain that you are going to find out how comments from different people are used in a biography. Explain that when comments are the actual words people have said, they are called **quotations**.

- Ask children to identify quotations in OHTs/posters 6 and 7 as you read them. Underline the quotations and explain that you are going to find out what they add to the meaning.

- Read paragraph 4 without the quotation (i.e. *After studying French and Classics at university, she worked for five years as a secretary. It was on a train journey to London at this time that the idea for Harry Potter first came to her*). Ask if this tells us what J.K. Rowling's thoughts and opinions were about being a secretary (no).

- Now read the quotation in paragraph 4, asking children what this adds (it tells the reader that she didn't particularly like being a secretary and what she did to make the time more enjoyable). This shows us something of J.K. Rowling's thoughts and feelings. It also tells us that she has always written stories and partly explains how she became a famous writer.

- Elicit what quotations from the subject can add to a biography (thoughts, feelings, opinions and personal details that no one else may know). Explain that quotations can also come from other people who knew the subject. Discuss other people who might be interviewed for J.K. Rowling's biography (e.g. her sister, who might talk about childhood memories of Joanne).

- Ensure children understand that they cannot just drop the quotations into the text; they need to introduce them using appropriate vocabulary either before or after the quotation (e.g. *"We badly wanted a rabbit," she remembers*; *"All I ever liked …" she recalls*).

- Look at the problems of using quotations – if the words are not reported exactly as they were spoken, how could this affect the meaning? If the J.K. Rowling quotation had been 'All I ever liked about working in offices was being able to type up stories on the computer', how does this alter the meaning? Compare it with the actual quotation.

- Tell children that you are going to look at a different type of comment used in biographies – that which **evaluates** the subject's achievements.

- To illustrate this, ask pairs of children to choose someone they both know. They each think of something about that person that has been especially successful – it could be something they have done, or something to do with the type of person they are. Explain that by doing this they are <u>evaluating</u> or judging what they think is successful about the person.

- Ask children to compare their thoughts and explain their choices. Discuss any differences in children's evaluations. Why might they have picked out different things about the same person? (everyone has different views on what is important or successful) Ask children to explain the reasons for their evaluations. Point out that whilst the evaluations are based on facts about the subject, they really are just the children's own personal **opinions**.

- Explain that in biographies, evaluative comments are usually found in the reorientation, after the facts have been presented.

- Ask children to identify the evaluative comments in the reorientation on OHT/poster 7 (*ability to hold her readers spellbound and eagerly awaiting the next book; … her skills as a storyteller*). Explain that we do not know if all readers feel like this about J.K. Rowling, so this is the author's opinion, not precise facts.

- Revise the point that reorientations may also include a reference to the subject's future, as this one does (*… does Harry Potter's biggest battle lie ahead? How will he stand the test of time …?*).

Group follow-up activities   1 red   pupil's book page 20   copymaster 3

Children decide where to place a selection of quotations in the Brunel biography. They discuss with a partner what the extra information adds for the reader.

Guided group support Help children to consider the relationship of the speaker to the subject. How might this have affected what they said? Ensure children understand that the quotations are speakers' opinions rather than hard facts.

2 blue   pupil's book page 20   copymaster 4

Children decide where to place a selection of quotations in the Spielberg biography. They discuss with a partner what the extra information adds for the reader.

Guided group support As for the red group. Alternatively, look at the use of tense in biographies and identify where and why it is used in this way.

3 yellow   pupil's book page 21

Children draw and complete a chart to show the contents of the reorientation from the Spielberg biography (the main aspect of life mentioned; the evaluative comments made; the writer's opinion).

Guided group support As for the red group. Alternatively, ask children to consider who the author might have approached to get quotations to flesh out the reorientation (e.g. a critic and an admirer of Spielberg).

Plenary Ask children to suggest what needs to be added to the 'How to write a biographical recount' poster under the headings 'Quotations' and 'Evaluative comments'. Recap what often goes in the reorientation section of biographies (e.g. evaluative comments about a key aspect of the subject; reference to the subject's future). Add this to the poster under the heading 'Reorientation'.

4 Planning the biography

Objectives To understand and form closed and open questions
To plan each section of the biography

Shared session *You need: 'Information' chart (from Session 1), OHT/poster 6, OHT/poster 8.*

In advance of Session 5 you will need to organise two people (e.g. parents, colleagues, friends) who are willing to be interviewed by the children as subjects for a biography. The first person is to be the subject for the shared session; the second is the subject for the red group's follow-up activity.

■ Tell children that they are going to learn how to interview a subject for a biography. Explain that they will be using the information from the interview to write a class biography.

■ Display the 'Information' chart from Session 1. Ask children, in pairs, to choose an information point and think of a question that could be asked to obtain that information (e.g. if the point is *published 1997*, the question might be 'When was your first book published?').

■ Discuss children's suggestions and write them in the left-hand column. Tell children that when the questions result in responses which give us specific pieces of information like those on the chart, they are called **closed questions**. Questions like this are used to collect key facts.

■ Now look at OHT/poster 6. Ask children to look at the information in paragraph 2 to identify where closed questions may have been used (e.g. to collect specific information about J.K. Rowling's place in the family, where she was born and when).

■ Explain that closed questions only provide limited information. For example, the question 'Did you like making up stories as a child?' would produce a yes/no answer which does not tell us much.

- Ask children to rephrase the question so that it would encourage J.K. Rowling to talk in more detail about her storytelling experiences (e.g. 'What can you remember about the time when you first started telling stories?').

- Explain that questions like this give the subject an opportunity to 'open up' and give us more information. They are called **open questions**.

- Ask children, again in pairs, to think of some open questions that would give J.K. Rowling the chance to talk freely or openly about:
  - her life at school;
  - any jobs she has done;
  - the ideas she had for her first book;
  - the publication of her books.

- Collect suggestions and discuss any questions that are rather vague (e.g. 'What was your childhood like?'). Explain that good open questions have a **focus**. Ask children to improve any vague questions by making them more focused.

- Display OHT/poster 8 and ask children to suggest what information they might want to include in each paragraph of the class biography. Can they suggest questions which would elicit that information from the subject? Write up a few of their suggestions. (You will be completing this activity in more detail in the plenary session.)

- Tell children they are now going to plan an interview for their own biographical recounts.

Group follow-up activities

If you feel children need more practice with identifying/ forming open and closed questions, there are differentiated activities on pages 22–23 of the pupil's book. You might want children to do these before preparing their own questions for the interview, using the questions in the pupil's book as models. Ensure that the completed copymasters are kept, as they will be needed in subsequent sessions.

red   copymaster 5   (pupil's book page 22 activity 1)

Tell children who they will be interviewing in Session 5 and ask them to plan open and closed questions to ask their subject.

Guided group support Reinforce children's understanding of the purpose of open and closed questions, when they are used and how to form them.

blue   copymaster 5   (pupil's book page 23 activity 2)

Children choose a modern, well-known personality and plan open and closed questions for this person.

Guided group support Help children to consider how they might phrase questions to encourage the subject to 'open up'.

yellow   copymaster 5   (pupil's book page 23 activity 3)

Children choose a historical character and plan open and closed questions for this person.

Guided group support Focus on real-life uses of open and closed questions (e.g. a news interview, a police interview, a celebrity interview). Ask children to consider why each type might be appropriate in each context.

Plenary

Display OHT/poster 8. Discuss the person who will be interviewed by the whole class in Session 5. What information do children want to find out about him/her? Ask for examples of closed questions from children's planning. Decide on the most suitable ones for this person – they will probably need adapting to be appropriate. Write these in the orientation section of the OHT/poster 8. Now do the same for the open questions, adding these to the key events section of the OHT/poster. Finally, think of a question for the reorientation section, such as 'What are your plans for the future?'

Plan how the interview will be conducted in Session 5, using the questions on OHT/poster 8, and deciding which questions different children will ask. Choose a child to greet the guest and another to thank the guest formally after the interview.

5 Researching the biography

Objectives

To carry out an interview using planned questions

To use researched information to plan a biographical recount

Shared session

You need: two interviewees, OHT/poster 8, different colour pen.

It may be helpful to make a video or audio recording of the interview. Explain that you can use this recording to check and edit the notes that will be taken during the interview. (A recording will also assist note-making in the follow-up activity below.)

■ Tell children that you are going to interview the subject for your class biography and make notes of the information collected. Briefly recap key points to remember when note-making.

■ Carry out the interview, with different children asking the questions you wrote up on OHT/poster 8 in the previous session.

■ Make notes of the interviewee's answers in the right-hand column on OHT/poster 8.

■ Tell children that they are now going to carry out research for their own biographies.

Group follow-up activities

red   copymaster 5

Children carry out the interview as arranged in the previous session. Ask one child to take notes, using the partially completed copymaster 5 from Session 4, or assume responsibility for this yourself.

Guided group support Help children add any additional information that is relevant but which might not easily match the prepared questions.

This activity requires some advance preparation. You will need to provide a range of reference materials, or arrange library/internet access. Alternatively, children can gather information as a homework activity.

blue/yellow   copymaster 5

Children use their planned questions to research answers from a variety of sources (interviews, articles, encyclopaedias, other biographies, the internet).

Guided group support As for the red group.

Plenary

Ask children to identify any difficulties that occurred during the research session and discuss suggestions for resolving the problems. Explain that biography writers use a variety of different research methods, just as the children have done. As well as interviewing the subject, they read other material that has been written about them (e.g. other interviews, articles, things the subject themselves may have written, what other people say about the subject).

6 Drafting the orientation

Objectives

To use a plan to draft the orientation of a biographical recount

To use connectives to link sentences

Shared session

You need: completed OHT/poster 8 (from Session 5), large sheet of paper, coloured pens, 'Connectives' chart (from Session 2), 'How to write a biographical recount' poster (from Session 1).

*See **Drafting** on page 7 for more detailed notes on conducting a whole-class drafting session.*

■ Tell the children that they are going to learn how to write an effective orientation for a biographical recount. Recap the purpose of orientations in biographical recounts (to give clear information about who the subject is and what is well known about them) and remind children of the intended reader.

■ Use the completed OHT/poster 8 from Session 5. Read through the information you gathered for the orientation and decide on the best order for it.

■ Using the first point, model the opening sentence on a large sheet of paper, explaining why you choose the words.

■ Take the next point and ask children, in pairs, to write it as a sentence, thinking about:

  ○ how to vary the opening words so the sentence does not begin with the subject's name;

  ○ who the readers will be and what they need to be told;

  ○ using a connective (if possible) at the beginning of the sentence to link it to the first sentence.

■ Ask for the children's suggestions and choose one to write up. Read through the sentence and discuss any changes needed. Then read both sentences together, looking at the flow of the text. Ask children for any suggestions to improve the flow, paying particular attention to the use of connectives.

■ Continue writing the orientation in this way, re-reading each sentence to ensure it fits with the flow of the whole paragraph. As you work, remind children of the needs of the reader, the importance of varying sentence beginnings and structures, and the need to use connectives where necessary to aid the flow (refer to the 'Connectives' chart from Session 2 if necessary).

■ Tell children that they are now going to draft an orientation for their own biographies.

Group follow-up activities   **red/blue/yellow**

Children use their research notes from Session 5 (copymaster 5) to draft their own orientation sections.

Guided group support

Red Help children to choose an appropriate connective to link two points in their orientation.

Blue Experiment with different ways of ordering the orientation. Encourage children to think of a variety of ways to begin their sentences.

Yellow Help children to vary sentence length, checking how well sentences read and flow and bearing in mind the reader's needs.

Plenary   Re-read the notes about orientations on your 'How to write a biographical recount' poster. Ask children if there are any changes or extra points they would like to include now they have drafted their own orientations. Ask for volunteers to read their orientations. Other children should listen and check that all the features are in place.

 Drafting the key events and reorientation sections

Objectives   To draft the key events and reorientation of a biographical recount

To use connective words and phrases to order events and link sentences

Shared session   *You need: OHTs/posters 6 and 7, completed OHT/poster 8 (from Session 5), large sheets of paper, coloured pens, 'Connectives' chart (from Session 2), 'How to write a biographical recount' poster (from Session 1), draft orientation.*

You may wish to teach this over two lessons, drafting the key events in the first and the reorientation in the second.

■ Tell children they are going to learn how to write effective key events and reorientation sections for a biography.

■ Read your notes in the key events section of OHT/poster 8 and, if necessary, sequence them to show the order in which they occurred.

■ Discuss appropriate words or phrases to convey the <u>first</u> aspect of the subject's life. Use the 'Connectives' chart to help you.

■ Ask the children, in pairs, to discuss how to form the opening sentence of the first paragraph. Discuss their ideas, choose one and write it on the class draft. Take suggestions for writing the remainder of the paragraph, using connectives to link sentences and a variety of sentence beginnings.

■ Repeat this for the remaining paragraphs of the key events section. When you have finished, read this section aloud for children to check that all the information is in place and that the text flows smoothly. Could any connectives be used to make smoother links between paragraphs?

■ Now consider the reorientation section. Recap that this section focuses on a key feature and often contains evaluative comments, based on the facts contained in the orientation and key events sections.

■ Identify the key feature of the subject to be focused upon in the reorientation – point out that the focus in the J.K. Rowling reorientation was on her success as a writer. Make an evaluation of this key feature. Recap how the J.K. Rowling evaluation considers her skills as a storyteller and the effect this has on her readers.

■ Remind children that in the reorientation, the author is summing up and offering their own opinion, based on the facts in the rest of the biography. Ask children to consider facts related to the identified key feature in your class biography, and to offer evaluative comments for the reorientation. Add one of these to your draft.

■ Ask children to think of a first sentence for the reorientation that evaluates the key feature identified. Decide on the best one for the draft.

■ If appropriate, consider the future of the subject. Recap how the J.K. Rowling reorientation questions how well her work will, in future, compare with the classics that have stood the test of time.

■ Ask children to think of a sentence to make a point about the subject's future and, again, use the best one. Discuss the use of a suitable connective word or phrase to introduce a change of idea or point (e.g. *however, but, unfortunately*).

■ Tell children that they are now going to draft the key events and reorientation sections of their own biographies.

Group follow-up activities   **red/blue/yellow**

Children draft the key events and reorientation sections of their biographies as demonstrated in the shared session.

Guided group support

Red Ensure that children think about each sentence before writing it and re-read their work as they write, making changes as necessary. Help children identify the key feature of their subject, to be focused on in the reorientation.

Blue Focus on the use of quotations and the vocabulary for introducing them (e.g. *recalls, remembers, reflects*). Help children evaluate their subject effectively.

Yellow Encourage children to present two opposing evaluations, which should be linked with an appropriate connective.

Plenary   Ask children to identify which aspects of the writing they found the most difficult. Ask if there is anything they want to add to the 'How to write a biographical recount' poster.

(8) Revising and editing the biographical recount

Objective To edit writing for sentence construction and meaning

Shared session *You need: class draft biography, coloured pen (different colour from those used in Session 7).*

*See **Revising and editing** on page 7 for more detailed advice.*

■ Tell children you are going to read the completed class biography to see if it can be improved, looking particularly at how well the points link together.

■ Divide the class into groups and give each a different revision focus:
   - using connectives to order events and link paragraphs, sentences and points within a sentence;
   - ensuring that all the information is included;
   - using a variety of sentence structures;
   - using quotations correctly;
   - checking that the text flows well;
   - checking whether the evaluation flows properly.

■ Read the biography aloud and take suggestions for improvement from each group, making any adjustments as necessary.

■ Tell children that they are going to revise and edit their own biographies.

Group follow-up activities **red/blue/yellow**

Children revise and edit their biographical recounts. They each read their completed biographies to a partner and receive feedback on:
   - how easy it is to follow the information;
   - how well the text flows;
   - how successfully they have included features of biographical recounts.

Guided group support

Red Focus on the children's use of connectives to order events and link paragraphs in their completed biographies.

Blue Focus on the children's use of connectives to link sentences in their completed biographies.

Yellow Focus on the children's use of connectives to link ideas within sentences in their completed biographies.

Plenary Ask for volunteers to read out their completed biographies and encourage the class to give constructive feedback.

(9) Publishing the biographical recount

Objectives To understand that there are different ways of publishing a biography

To use additional pictorial material to support the textual information

Shared session *You need: range of published biographies, revised class or child's biography, large sheet of paper, coloured pens.*

*See **Publishing** on page 8 for more detailed notes on the issues involved in the final presentation of the text.*

If possible, supply some photographs of the subject for use in the published version of the class biography.

■ Tell children that you are going to plan the layout of the class biography, adding illustrations or diagrams where possible.

■ Give children a range of biographies to look at. Focus on:
  ○ how the orientation, key events and reorientation sections are arranged. Does each section begin on a new page? How are headings used to help the reader? Where are illustrations or diagrams used?
  ○ the front and back covers. How are they set out? What is included, and where? (e.g. pictures, title, author) How do they attract potential readers?
  ○ information about the author of the biography (if any). Where is it? What does it contain?

■ Use the revised class biography or one of the children's biographies. Demonstrate how to prepare the finished version – ask for suggestions about:
  ○ how the sections will be arranged on each page;
  ○ how any pictorial information can be used;
  ○ the design of the front and back covers;
  ○ where information about the authors can be positioned.

■ Draw a rough layout plan on a large sheet of paper, showing which sections go where and the position of any illustrations.

■ Tell children they are now going to plan how to publish their own biographies.

Group follow-up activities **red/blue/yellow**

Children work on publishing their biographies, as demonstrated in the shared session.

Guided group support

Red Help children to plan the layout of their biographies, bearing in mind the needs of the reader.

Blue Focus on the use of diagrams or timelines to help the reader understand where information in the biography fits into the subject's life overall.

Yellow Identify how different textual features can be used to assist the reader (e.g. italics, bold print, capital letters, different fonts, different size print).

Plenary Ask children to identify any difficulties they had publishing their biographies. Discuss how these could be resolved. Each child should display and read their biography to a partner and receive feedback on its presentation.

ADDITIONAL SESSIONS

Descriptions from different perspectives

Objectives To understand that the subject will be viewed differently in different situations

To understand that the descriptions of the subject will be affected by who the writer is, the writer's purpose and the intended reader

Shared session *You need: OHT/posters 6 and 7, OHT/poster 9, large sheet of paper, coloured pens.*

- Explain that you are going to look at J.K. Rowling from different points of view.

- Ask children to think of times when someone has talked or written about them (e.g. a friend to another friend, a parent in a letter, a teacher in a report).

- Discuss possible differences between the views expressed at these times (e.g. a friend might describe you from a social viewpoint as being fun to be with, a teacher might focus on your work and describe you as hardworking or lazy, a parent might be proud of you all round, in terms of social skills, schoolwork and how you behave at home). Ensure that children remember that people who are close to them, such as members of their family, may be biased!

- Explain that you are going to look at three descriptions of the same person, written from different points of view. Display and read OHT/poster 9. Ask children to identify where the three descriptions come from (personal letter, school report, character reference). Now ask them to identify for each one:
    - the purpose;
    - the intended reader;
    - the style – formal or informal?
    - the content – what aspects of the character does it focus on?

- Now tell children you are going to write some descriptions from different perspectives. Write the opening two sentences of a school report for J.K. Rowling. Ask children who would be writing this (her teacher). Which aspects of her would the teacher be focusing on? (How well she works at school, how she relates to her classmates.) What would the style be? (formal)

- Then write two sentences of a personal letter from a school friend to a cousin, explaining why you are writing about J.K. Rowling (e.g. she has been entertaining you and some friends with stories during lunchtime). What aspects should you focus on? What will the style be here? (informal)

- Finally, write two sentences of a character reference for J.K. Rowling (e.g. she works for you as a secretary but has applied for another secretarial job). What aspects should you focus on? What will the style be? (formal)

- Ask children what impression we get of J.K. Rowling's character if we look at these pieces of writing in isolation.

Group follow-up activities **1 red   pupil's book page 24   copymaster 6**

Children continue writing the school report for J.K. Rowling. They use the extracts from J.K. Rowling's biography and autobiography in the pupil's book to help them.

Guided group support Help children to identify the aspects of J.K. Rowling that will feature in a school report (e.g. attitude to work, behaviour, relationships with others, abilities, interests) and to use formal language.

2 blue   pupil's book page 25

Children continue writing the personal letter about J.K. Rowling. They use the extracts from J.K. Rowling's biography and autobiography to help them.

Guided group support Help children to focus on the aspects of J.K. Rowling that will feature in the letter (e.g. the stories she tells, when, what they like/dislike about her, what they feel about her skills, what sort of person she is).

3 yellow   pupil's book page 25

Children continue writing the character reference for J.K. Rowling. They use an extract from J.K. Rowling's biography to help them.

Guided group support Help children to focus on the aspects of J.K. Rowling that will feature in the reference (what she does well/does not do well in the job, how well she gets on with her colleagues, how reliable and conscientious she is, her attitude to her work).

Plenary Ask volunteers to read aloud their character descriptions. Ask the other children what aspect of J.K. Rowling is being focused upon each time, and to identify similarities and differences in what is being said about her. What might they think of J.K. Rowling if they had only read one of these descriptions? Ensure children understand that, in order to get a balanced picture of the person, we need to look at all the descriptions together.

Writing in a journalistic style

Objectives To understand that journalistic writing needs to present balanced views and needs to consider the readers' interests

To rewrite a section of biographical writing in journalistic style

Shared session *You need: OHTs/posters 6 and 7, OHT/poster 10, large sheet of paper, coloured pens.*

■ Tell children that they are going to learn how to write like a journalist.

■ Discuss why people read newspapers and magazines. Ask children which papers they get at home. Do they read them?

■ Ask what the purpose of a newspaper report is (to convey information about events happening in the world). Discuss with children what problems there would be if a journalist wrote only his/her opinions in a newspaper report (this presents only one view, and could influence some readers). Do children think this is fair or not? Explain that good reporting provides a mixture of fact and opinion.

■ Tell children they are going to read a part of a newspaper report about J.K. Rowling. They are going to investigate this report to see how well the journalist has balanced facts with their opinions.

■ Display OHT/poster 10. Ask half the class to look for facts and half to look for opinions as you read it. Then discuss their findings and list them. For example:

Opinion	Fact
She is a wizard at storytelling.	She is a famous writer.
She is entertaining.	She told stories to her younger sister.
She has a creative gift.	Her sister's name is Di.
She writes imaginative stories.	Some of her stories were about things she did not have.
Her stories helped her enjoy experiences missing in her real world.	

■ Ask children to think about the balance of opinions and facts. Are all the opinions fair? Can any be challenged? (It is misleading to say that her stories helped her to enjoy experiences missing in her real world as we only know of one missing experience – not having a rabbit.)

■ Now ask children to think about the writer's main message in the report (J.K. Rowling has always had a good imagination and has enjoyed sharing this).

■ Note that the style of this report is quite informal. Point out the puns *wizard at storytelling* and *conjure up a world of her own*. Children should understand that other newspapers might have a more serious style than this. Ensure that children can see that the facts are conveyed as concisely as possible, without taking up too much space or losing the reader's attention.

■ Explain that you are going to write the next paragraph for the same newspaper report. Display and re-read OHTs/posters 6 and 7. Ask children to suggest which part may be of interest to a newspaper reader (e.g. when she wrote her first *Harry Potter* book sitting in cafés to keep warm).

■ Identify the main message for this paragraph. Write it at the top of a large sheet of paper for reference. Ask children to suggest the points to be made in order to convey this message, and list these in note form.

■ Model writing the first sentence, explaining that it needs to give the essential point of the paragraph and should be fair. Ask for suggestions on how to finish the rest of the paragraph, concentrating on:

  ○ clear, uncomplicated sentences to keep the reader's attention;
  ○ balancing fact and opinion;
  ○ ensuring opinions are fair;
  ○ ensuring it is of interest to readers.

■ When you have finished, re-read the paragraph, asking children to check it has all these features.

Group follow-up activities

1 red   pupil's book page 26

Children write a paragraph for a newspaper report on Isambard Kingdom Brunel using the information in the pupil's book.

Guided group support Help children to plan and write the first sentence so that it conveys the essential point of the paragraph.

2 blue   pupil's book page 27

Children identify facts and opinions in a newspaper report on Steven Spielberg. They consider the balance and fairness of the writing and its interest for readers.

Guided group support Ensure children understand what is meant by a fair point (i.e. one that is clearly supported by evidence).

3 yellow   pupil's book page 27   copymaster 4

Children choose a paragraph in the Steven Spielberg biography and rewrite it in journalistic style.

Guided group support Focus on the structure of sentences. Help children write sentences that do not contain too many subordinate clauses.

Plenary

Ask children to explain what they understand by journalistic style (e.g. balance, fairness, uncomplicated style, giving essential information in the first sentence). Write up their comments on a class poster entitled 'How to write in a journalistic style'. Ask for volunteers to read their reports aloud. Encourage the other children to give constructive feedback.

Writing a newspaper report

Objectives
To reinforce understanding of the features of newspaper reports

To consider differences between standard English and sensational journalese

To write a newspaper report

Shared session
You need: OHTs/posters 6 and 7 (optional), large sheets of paper, coloured pens, examples of newspaper reports, 'How to write in a journalistic style' poster (from previous session).

 You may wish to teach this additional session over two lessons.

- ■ Tell children that you are going to write a short newspaper report about an event in the J.K. Rowling biography.

- ■ Revise the structure of newspaper reports (headline, orientation, main body, reorientation, possibly an accompanying photo and caption). Show children some examples if possible.

- ■ Ask children to choose an event from the J.K. Rowling biography that would have made an interesting read when it occurred (e.g. when her books first sold a million copies in Britain). Explain that you are going to plan and write a newspaper report about this event.

- ■ Start with the orientation. Recap the information this should contain (who?, what?, where?, when?, why?, how?). Note children's suggestions on a large sheet of paper.

- ■ Demonstrate how to write the orientation. Explain that in newspaper reports, this is often a single sentence.

- ■ Ask children to list the points to be covered in the main body of the report. Write these up and number them in order of importance – this is the order in which they will appear.

- ■ Now write the main body of the report with the children. As you write, explain that the sentences need to be in a clear, uncomplicated style. Ask children for connectives to link points within the paragraph, and to link each paragraph. Refer to the 'How to write in a journalistic style' chart as you work.

- ■ Now revise what children know about newspaper headlines (they are usually written as short, dramatic sentences or phrases which 'hook' the reader).

- ■ Ask for examples of words that relate to J.K. Rowling's books and have a double meaning (e.g. *spell*, *conjure*, *wizard*). Ask children to play with these words and, with a partner, to think of a catchy headline that also sums up the story (e.g. MAGICIAN SPELLS SUCCESS FOR WRITER). Discuss which is the best one and write it at the top of the report.

- ■ Explain that some newspaper reports are written in a **sensational** style. Ask children what they think this means (e.g. it stirs up great public excitement/interest, sometimes by exaggerating the facts). Discuss which newspapers use this style.

- ■ Tell children that you are going to rewrite the orientation of the class report, using more sensational language. Model the first sentence, for example:

    Fearless wizard Harry Potter soared to fame from impoverished beginnings in an Edinburgh café.

    Point out some of the language features used here (e.g. clichés like *soared to fame*; use of very strong vocabulary, such as *impoverished* instead of *poor*).

- ■ If time permits, ask children to help you finish this paragraph.

Group follow-up activities

Allow children to use the 'How to write in a journalistic style' poster to help them if necessary.

1 red   pupil's book page 28

Children change given headlines to a more sensational style.

Guided group support Help children use alternative words and word order to make the greatest impact.

2 blue   pupil's book page 29

Children change a paragraph from a newspaper report about Steven Spielberg from standard English to a sensational tabloid style.

Guided group support Focus on reordering words until the desired effect is created.

3 yellow   pupil's book page 29   copymaster 4

Children select a newsworthy event from the Steven Spielberg biography. They write this as an orientation for a newspaper report, firstly in standard English and then in a sensational tabloid style.

Guided group support Focus on the use of exaggerated language for the sensational style and identify whether or not the impression it gives the reader is accurate.

Plenary Ask children to summarise key features of a sensational journalistic style, giving examples from the reports they wrote in their group activities.

Writing a CV

Objectives To understand the purpose and organisation of a CV

To extract relevant information for a CV from a variety of sources

To write a CV for the subject of the biography

Shared session *You need: a variety of CVs (real or made up), OHTs/posters 6 and 7, large sheet of paper, coloured pens.*

- Tell children that they are going to learn how to write a CV.

- Explain that 'CV' is an abbreviation of *curriculum vitae* which is Latin for 'the course of one's life'. A CV is a list of information about a person, usually covering their education, qualifications, previous jobs and interests. Explain when and why CVs are used (to tell people about yourself when applying for jobs or courses).

- If possible, show children a variety of CVs. Ask what they notice about the headings, layout and the type of print.

- Ask children to identify headings for a CV and note these (e.g. name, address, date of birth, marital status, education, qualifications, previous occupations, hobbies).

- Explain that you are going to prepare a CV for J.K. Rowling. Point out that some of the information will not be available to the children.

- Ask children to suggest an order for the headings on the CV. Number your list accordingly. Discuss:
  - exact wording for the headings;
  - where to position them;
  - what type and size of print to use.

Write the headings up as a framework on a large sheet of paper.

■ Display OHTs/posters 6 and 7 alongside the CV framework. Collect any information about J.K. Rowling which could be included on her CV. Write it under the appropriate heading on the framework. Discuss where missing information could be found using other resources.

■ Tell children that they are going to design some CV frameworks themselves.

Group follow-up activities   **red   copymasters 3 and 7**

Children use the information on copymaster 3 and the framework on copymaster 7 to write a CV for Brunel.

Guided group support Help children to position the information correctly in the framework.

blue   copymaster 4

Children design a CV framework and add Steven Spielberg's details.

Guided group support Help children to identify and use other sources to find any missing information. If possible, give them some example CVs to evaluate.

yellow

Children use ICT to design a CV framework using a variety of text and layout features.

Guided group support Help children to make best possible use of layout and text features. If possible, give them some example CVs to evaluate.

Plenary   Ask children to explain what they have learnt about preparing a CV. Discuss the difficulties of preparing a CV for another person.

Ask children in the yellow group to show the CV frameworks they have designed. Ask for feedback from the class on their choice of headings, layout and print features.

 ## Homework suggestions

○ Make a collection of connectives from your reading. Separate them into those that link:
  • events between paragraphs;
  • sentences within paragraphs;
  • points within a sentence.
  (After Session 2)

○ Plan, research and write the biography of Queen Victoria or someone else you have read about in history lessons. **(After Session 7)**

○ Interview an older relative, then plan and write their biography. **(After Session 7)**

○ Write an author blurb to go with your biography. Write about:

  • why you chose this person as your subject;
  • key facts about <u>your</u> own life (family, hobbies, achievements, school career).
  (After Session 9)

○ Continue writing the newspaper report your teacher began with the whole class. **(After 'Writing in a journalistic style')**

○ Make a collection of sensational and serious newspaper reports on the same subject. Compare differences in the language that is used.
  (After 'Writing a newspaper report')

○ Write your own CV or a CV for a character in a book you have read. **(After 'Writing a CV')**

UNIT 2   How to write a biographical recount

Colour the right number of stars to show how well you did the following things:

0 stars = I didn't do it.
1 star = I gave it a try.
2 stars = I did it quite well.

3 stars = I did it well.
4 stars = I did an excellent job!

I used open and closed questions to collect my information.	☆	☆	☆	☆
I planned my recount with an orientation, key events and a reorientation.	☆	☆	☆	☆
I wrote an orientation that introduced key facts about the subject.	☆	☆	☆	☆
I organised the key events in chronological order.	☆	☆	☆	☆
I wrote an evaluative comment in the reorientation.	☆	☆	☆	☆
I used a variety of time connective words and phrases.	☆	☆	☆	☆
I used quotations to add extra interesting information.	☆	☆	☆	☆
I improved my writing by revising it.	☆	☆	☆	☆
I presented my biography in an interesting way.	☆	☆	☆	☆

Something I am especially pleased with

Something my audience liked in my writing

Something I'd like to do better next time

Term two fiction focus:
3 How to write a mystery story with flashbacks

What most children will already know:

The narrative structure of a story – beginning, middle, end

That stories contain problems, conflicts, climaxes and resolutions

The importance of chronological order

How to write a story in chapters

How to show characterisation through dialogue and action

What children will learn in this unit:

The conventions of a mystery story

To use the language of mystery stories

To write flashbacks

To plan stories to include flashbacks

---

1 What makes a detective mystery?

Objectives To understand the conventions of a mystery story

Shared session *You need: OHT/poster 11, a large sheet of paper, coloured pens.*

This unit concentrates on detective mystery stories, in which the mystery is solved at the end of the story. Children should have experience of reading detective mysteries and other stories containing flashbacks.

■ Tell children that they will be learning how to write a detective mystery that includes flashbacks.

■ Display and read OHT/poster 11. Explain that it is a review of a detective mystery. Ask children to underline key features of the story. Make a class poster entitled 'What makes a detective mystery?'. (If you wish, follow the layout of copymaster 8.) List the key features on the poster.

■ Ask about the **central mystery** in the story (the discovery of Benjamin Fisher's body). Explain that the plot hinges on this mystery, which we are made aware of right at the beginning of the story.

■ Ask who tries to find out what happened (Candy and Jake). Explain that they are the **detectives** (the people in the story who are trying to solve the mystery).

■ Ask children to pick out names of other people (Katherine and Kieran Eastwood, Ted Johnstone, Arthur Rathbone and the postwoman). They are **suspects** (people suspected of committing the crime).

■ Ask why these people might have wanted to kill Benjamin Fisher. List responses under **motives**, emphasising that a suspect must have a strong reason for wanting to commit the crime (e.g. love, money).

■ Ask how Candy and Jake find out that the killer is Arthur Rathbone and list the **clues** they find (the discovery that Arthur Rathbone was a martial arts expert, the newspaper cutting).

■ Ask if all the clues point to Arthur Rathbone, or if there are any that throw the investigators off the track (e.g. the illegal brandy). Explain that a clue that reveals no evidence and diverts attention from the truth is called a **red herring**.

- Ask what finally convinces Jake and Candy that Arthur Rathbone is the murderer (the kettle painting). This is the **evidence** which proves who committed the crime.

- Finally, ask children to identify other mystery conventions from their own reading, TV or films. Add these to the class poster. For example:

  - **Witness**: someone who sees, or can give information about, the crime. In a detective mystery, all witnesses are usually suspects – unless they have an alibi.

  - **Alibi:** a suspect's claim that they were somewhere else when the crime was committed. Sometimes an alibi is a person, who will state that the suspect was with them at the time of the crime, and not at the scene. Detectives have to check whether alibis are genuine.

  - **Resolution:** the final part of the story, in which the evidence is explained, the culprit and their motives are revealed and the mystery is solved.

Group follow-up activities

A grid for children to copy and complete is given in the pupil's book. Alternatively, children could use copymaster 8 to list the key features.

If children use copymaster 8, they should add extra boxes entitled 'Witness(es)', 'Alibi(s)', 'Red herring(s)'.

1 red   pupil's book pages 30–31   (copymaster 8)

Children identify key features of *The Mystery of the Missing Painting*, or another detective mystery that they have read recently.

Guided group support Reiterate the main conventions of a detective mystery and ensure that children understand them. Ensure children see that the detective needs to look for clues to solve the crime.

2 blue/yellow   pupil's book page 31   (copymaster 8)

Children identify the key features of a detective mystery they have read in guided or independent reading.

Guided group support

Blue As with the red group. Ensure children understand the concept of a 'red herring'.

Yellow As with the red group. Focus on the role of a witness and the importance of checking alibis.

Plenary Choose a group to present their findings to the class. Use their findings to reinforce the main conventions needed when writing a mystery story.

② How to use flashbacks in a story

Objectives To understand the concept of a flashback

To investigate ways of putting flashbacks into stories

Shared session *You need: a large sheet of paper, coloured pens, OHT/poster 12.*

- Tell children that you are going to find out how authors write flashbacks. Prepare a class poster entitled 'How to write flashbacks'. Use it throughout the session to compile a chart that children will find useful when writing.

- Ask children what a **flashback** is (the part of a story that recalls an incident that happened in the past). Explain that in a flashback, the narrative moves from the present day to the past. After the flashback, the narrative returns to the present.

- Ask why flashbacks are used in detective mysteries (to reveal more clues or to bring all the clues together and solve the case).

- Display and read OHT/poster 12. Ask how the author moves into the flashback (by using a diary extract written in the past, which one of the characters reads). Ask if this is an effective way of revealing clues and evidence (yes, especially if it is a murder mystery and the diary belongs to the victim or a suspect). Explain that **documentary evidence** (written evidence) is especially useful.

- Discuss the way the author moves into the flashback by using one of the 'detectives' to read the diary. Look at the way the flashback ends (with the end of the diary entry) and returns to the present.

- Ask children to list some different kinds of flashback (characters' memories, recounts, letters, newspaper reports, audio- or video-tape recordings). Give two examples of how these might be used in detective mysteries, for example:

  - The detective could ask the suspect to describe what happened; the suspect would then give a recount. The flashback would then return to the present with the detective thanking the suspect for the statement and ending the interview.

  - A 'story within a story' could be used to describe something that happened to one of the suspects in the past, revealing why they might have wanted to commit the crime.

Group follow-up activities

1 red   pupil's book page 32

Children write another diary entry for Benjamin Fisher.

Guided group support Help children to move fluently between past and present. Encourage them to bring different settings into the flashback.

2 blue/yellow   pupil's book pages 32–33

Children read the extract from 'Truth or Dare' and write the next chapter using one of the flashback techniques they have learnt.

Guided group support As with the red group.

This is a good activity to precede writing flashbacks as it gives children a related 'speaking and listening' experience.

3 red/blue/yellow   pupil's book pages 34–35

If time permits, children work in mixed ability groups of six to give oral flashback accounts of a robbery. One child plays the detective, the others play the suspects. The suspects decide which one of them is guilty. The 'detective' asks each suspect to give a flashback account of what they were doing when the crime was committed. After the flashbacks have been given, the detective questions the suspects and identifies the thief.

Plenary Ask children what they have learnt about flashbacks (they move the narrative temporarily from the present into the past; they can reveal clues and evidence about a crime). Ask some children to share their flashback writing, and/or others to report back on the oral activity.

③ The language of mystery stories

Objectives To develop the use of settings

To compile a bank of words and phrases to create atmosphere and build suspense

Shared session *You need: OHT/poster 13, coloured pens, a large sheet of paper.*

62

- Explain that you are going to investigate vocabulary used in detective mysteries to help children write their own stories. Make a class poster entitled 'Mysterious words and phrases'. Add to this throughout the session to create a class word bank for children to use in their own writing.

- Tell them they are going to read an extract from the beginning of Anne Fine's book *Step by Wicked Step* where the author has created an atmosphere of mystery and suspense. Display and read OHT/poster 13 and ask children to identify what makes the setting mysterious.

- Underline in one colour all the words in the passage that describe Old Harwick Hall (*haunted, overgrown driveway, looming hole, peeling sign, vast staircase, huge, echoing mansion*). Ask what kind of atmosphere these words create.

- Discuss the author's choice of adjectives and their effects. For example, the driveway is *overgrown*, implying it is unused and encouraging the reader to wonder why.

- Focus on *Fronds of strange plants* ... to ... *oil-painted eyes*. Ask how the author makes objects appear mysterious. Cover her use of:
  - adjectives (e.g. *strange, disturbed, hardened*);
  - verbs to personify objects by describing them as doing things (*stretched from their pots, fingered them, chattered, stared*).

- Point out that stormy weather is often used to create atmosphere. Underline in a different colour all the weather words and phrases (*the night had turned wild, peal of thunder, rain-spattered windows, livid flash of lightning*). Ask children what they notice (the storm is getting worse). Discuss how the author builds up suspense by simultaneously increasing the power of the storm.

- Underline *flickered, shiver, peered anxiously* in the first paragraph. Discuss the effects of these words (they create an atmosphere of suspense). Substitute different verbs and note the effect (e.g. *Each peal of thunder made the map in Mr Plumley's hand move/wiggle*). The word *move* is nondescript; the word *wiggle* would make the sentence comic.

Group follow-up activities

1 red   pupil's book page 36

Children complete the cloze passage on their own by using 'mystery' words from the word box, or from the class word bank created in the shared session. They then compare their work with a partner's.
Guided group support Help children choose appropriate vocabulary to create a mysterious atmosphere. Discuss reasons for choices.

2 blue   pupil's book page 37

In the pupil's book, children read a continuation of the extract you read together on OHT/poster 3. Using words/phrases from the class word bank created in the shared session, they describe orally to a partner what might lie behind the door. They then write the next paragraph of the story, trying to create a mysterious atmosphere.

Guided group support Ensure children pair adjectives and nouns in an interesting way.

3 yellow   pupil's book page 37

Children look at the boat picture and orally describe the setting to a partner. They then write about the events on board, trying to create a mysterious atmosphere.

Guided group support Encourage use of a wide range of unusual adjectives/adjectival phrases.

Alternative group activity   **red/blue/yellow**

Children use stories they have read to search for words and phrases that create a mysterious atmosphere. Encourage them to make a personal word bank.

Plenary   Ask children what they have learnt about creating a mysterious atmosphere in a detective mystery. Ask volunteers to contribute more mysterious words/phrases to the class word bank.

4 Planning the mystery

Objectives   To plan a mystery story, using the conventions of mystery story writing

To identify settings and relationships between characters

Shared session   *You need: OHT/poster 14, a large sheet of paper, coloured pens, copymasters 9 and 10.*

- Tell the children you are going to write a clear, easy-to-follow plan for a class detective mystery.

- Point out that detective mysteries are often set in the locality where the detective is based. Suggest that the class detective story is also based on a local area (e.g. your town, village or housing estate) or local community (e.g. the football team, swimming club). Establish your audience.

- Choose one of the following stimuli and use it as a starting point for planning the class mystery in note form:
  - a wallet or jewellery box with items missing; a picture in a frame; a diary or letter;
  - a newspaper headline;
  - a 'scene of the crime' that you have already set up in school. Leave on the floor, as if abandoned, an empty cashbox or the disconnected leads of a missing computer. Clues may be found around the room (e.g. an open window, fingerprints, footprints, an initialled pen, an article of clothing, a diary).

- Display the 'Mystery planning chart' on OHT/poster 14 and:
  - make notes on the central mystery;
  - choose a name for the detective and decide on their character;
  - fill in the 'Setting' box. If appropriate, plan two settings or a change of atmosphere for the setting during the flashback;
  - complete the 'Clues' section by discussing the clues left at the scene of the crime;
  - decide on the name, age and character of each suspect;
  - identify a motive for each suspect;
  - decide which suspect is guilty and mark their name with a star;
  - tell children that it is important that the author knows who the culprit is, even though this will not be revealed until the end of the story;
  - think of a title for the mystery.

- Read through the 'Mystery planning chart' together and keep it for use in future sessions.

- Tell children they are now going to plan their own detective mysteries.

Group follow-up activities   **1 red**   pupil's book page 38   copymaster 9

Children can work individually or in pairs. If they work individually, they will be asked to tell a partner how their plan works.

Children plan their own detective mystery based on a picture story.

Guided group support Plan the story as a group, or have part of the copymaster already filled in (e.g. the clues and names of the suspects). Help children decide which clue implicates each suspect and write it in the 'Clues' box on the suspect profile.

2 blue   pupil's book page 39   copymaster 9

Children plan a detective mystery including two suspects and related clues.

Guided group support Ask children to include a clue that is a 'red herring'.

3 yellow   pupil's book page 39   copymaster 10

Children choose one of the stimuli and plan a detective mystery including three suspects and a flashback with a contrasting setting.

Guided group support Encourage children to draw arrows between the 'Suspect' boxes to indicate any relationship between people in the story, writing the relationship on the arrow.

Plenary   Ask children what they have learnt. Write responses on a large sheet of paper entitled 'How to write mystery stories'. Keep this chart for future use (you will be adding to it during subsequent plenary sessions). Ask children to describe their story plans.

(5) Planning the plot

Objectives   To plan a plot for a mystery story

To manipulate the plot plan to include flashbacks

Shared session   *You need: completed OHT/poster 14 (from Session 4), copymaster 11 (for reference), a large sheet of paper, coloured pens.*

- Display the completed OHT/poster 14 from Session 4 and recap. Tell children you are now going to plan the plot for the class mystery.

- Revise the structure of a story plan (beginning, middle, end) and the purpose of each part. Following the layout of copymaster 11, write headings for your 'Plot plan' on a large sheet of paper. Tell children you are going to use this as your outline, but you are going to make some additions (e.g. flashbacks).

- Plan the beginning. Discuss which characters children wish to introduce first. Decide on setting. Plan the central mystery, explaining that it must be introduced early, to entice the audience. Decide how to set the scene.

- Make notes on the end of the story. Ensure children understand that this must solve the mystery, revealing to the other characters <u>who</u> committed the crime and <u>why</u>.

- Now plan the middle of the story. First plan the **climax** (when all the clues come together and the guilty suspect is identified). In traditional detective mysteries this often occurs when a piece of conclusive evidence is revealed. It might take the form of a confession, or could involve a flashback, with the detective, or a witness, taking everyone 'back in time' to reveal what actually happened.

■ Next, plan the part that leads up to the climax. Its main thrust will be to introduce the suspects and their motives so that the climax can reveal who committed the crime. Each suspect's motives must be made clear. To maintain suspense, no suspect can be discounted until the climax. A simple way to introduce suspects is for the detective to interview them. Each suspect could provide a recount of the crime as a flashback, at the same time revealing their motives. Plan a flashback using the box on the right of the plan. Add extra boxes if needed.

■ Finally, read through the completed 'Plot plan' and ensure that everything has been included. Invite a group to act out the story. This exposes any faults before the first draft is written and is a fun way to end. If, during the acting out, it becomes obvious that parts of the plot do not make sense, demonstrate how they can be changed.

■ Discuss the use of chapters in a story, and mark on the plan where they should begin and end. Keep the 'Plot plan' for use in Session 6.

■ Tell children they are going to write their own 'Plot plans'.

Group follow-up activities

To help them, children should use the 'Mystery planning chart' completed on OHT/poster 14 during Session 4. Encourage them to discuss their plots as they work, and explain them to another person to ensure that they make sense. They could work in groups to act out each other's mysteries, with the person who planned the story acting as 'director'.

 red copymaster 11

Children plan their mystery plot, including one flashback at the climax.

Guided group support Help children focus on planning in paragraphs. Further support could be given if necessary by planning the story as a group.

 blue copymaster 11

Children plan their mystery plot, adding one more box to the 'Flashbacks' column.

Guided group support Ensure children's plots are clear. Help children to include flashbacks, ensuring that they make sense.

 yellow copymaster 11

Children plan their mystery plot, adding two or three more boxes to the 'Flashbacks' column.

Guided group support Focus on structuring the story in clear chapters.

Plenary Ask children what they have learnt about planning a mystery story. Write responses on the 'How to write mystery stories' chart from Session 4. Invite volunteers to describe their plans and/or act out their plots. Ask others to observe and assess whether they make sense.

6 Drafting the beginning of the story

Objectives To draft the beginning of a story, using the 'hook' of the central mystery to entice the reader

To follow a story plan, and modify it if necessary

Shared session *You need: OHT/poster 15, 'Mysterious words and phrases' poster (from Session 3), completed OHT/poster 14 (from Session 4), 'Plot plan' (from Session 5), a large sheet of paper, coloured pens.*

■ Tell children they are going to learn how to write a good beginning to their detective mysteries.

■ Display OHT/poster 15. Recap on what makes a good beginning (detectives and central mystery – discovery of the body – introduced straight away, making reader want to continue). Ask children to identify words used to build suspense (*dead body, abandoned, black, swirling depths, sightless face, long, long dead*).

■ Write the beginning of the class mystery, referring back to the 'Plot plan' and completed OHT/poster 14. Use words from the 'Mysterious words and phrases' poster created in Session 3.

■ As you write, revise paragraphing. Note and explain use of each new paragraph.

■ Refer to your notes on chapter structure in the 'Plot plan', and ask children if they have ideas about how each chapter should end. Explain that chapters often end with **cliffhangers** that draw the reader on. Ask children to recall cliffhangers in stories they have read. Try to include cliffhangers in the chapter endings of your shared writing.

■ Tell children they are going to write the beginning of their own mysteries.

Group follow-up activities

red/blue/yellow

Children use the plot plans they created in Session 5 to draft the beginning of their own stories. They should use the 'Mysterious words and phrases' chart from Session 3 to help them.

Guided group support

Red Help children to write a story beginning that introduces the main characters and the mystery.

Blue Help children to write a story beginning in paragraphs that provide a 'hook' for the rest of the story and include some 'mystery' vocabulary.

Yellow Encourage children to write a story beginning that immediately involves the reader, and builds suspense.

Plenary

Ask children to read out their story beginnings. Set each group a 'listening target' as follows for evaluating the effectiveness of each:

- Red: has the central mystery been introduced?
- Blue: does the beginning contain 'mystery' vocabulary?
- Yellow: does the beginning build suspense and provide a 'hook' for the rest of the story?

7 Drafting the middle and the end of the story

Objectives

To draft the middle and end of a detective mystery, following a plan

To use specific vocabulary to build suspense throughout the story

To use flashbacks

Shared session

You need: 'Mysterious words and phrases' poster (from Session 3), completed OHT/poster 14 (from Session 4), 'Plot plan' (from Session 5), 'How to write mystery stories' poster (from Session 4), a large sheet of paper, coloured pens.

 See **Drafting** on page 7 for more detailed advice on conducting a whole-class drafting session.

■ Tell children you are going to draft the middle and end of your mystery story. Display completed OHT/poster 14, the 'Mystery planning chart', and the 'Plot plan'.

2 You may want to spread this over two shared sessions – one for the middle and one for the end. Alternatively, you may wish to use a longer extended writing session.

■ Re-read the beginning of your story and look at your 'Plot plan' for the middle section.

■ Discuss how each chapter might end with a cliffhanger. Write children's ideas for cliffhangers on the plan.

■ Continue with shared writing, following the plan. Write each chapter in a different colour to emphasise structure. Use another colour to highlight the 'hook' which draws the reader into the story.

■ Invite ideas on how to pad out the story. Refer back to the suspects on the 'Mystery planning chart'. Ask how their characters will be revealed (through flashbacks, dialogue, action, or by the narrator). Ask children to suggest words from the poster to help to create atmosphere and build suspense.

■ Tick off each part of the plan as you write. Ensure that all motives and clues have been revealed in the story ending.

■ Explain that children are now going to continue with their own stories. First they will need to re-read the beginning of their story, and refer to their own plot plan.

Group follow-up activities

red/blue/yellow

Children draft the middle and end of their stories.

Guided group support

Red Help children to follow their story plan and write the flashback.

Blue Help children to follow their story plan and include all planned elements, including two flashbacks. Ensure that they use mystery vocabulary to build suspense.

Yellow Focus on building suspense through the successive chapters, leading up to the climax. Ensure that children control the flashbacks effectively.

Plenary Ask what children have learnt about writing a detective mystery. Add their comments to the 'How to write mystery stories' poster from Session 4. Discuss the usefulness of a plot plan and ask if anyone changed theirs as they were writing. Look at plans that have been changed and discuss why.

Ask children to read a successful part of their story, giving reasons as to why it is well written (e.g. mysterious setting described, interesting words used). After each reading, invite positive comments and suggest one point for improvement.

8 Revising and editing the story

Objectives To understand that writing can be improved by going back to it and working on it again

To consider the main points about writing mystery stories and to check that these have been included in the writing

To ensure that the plot makes sense

To ensure that flashbacks have been included

Shared session *You need: 'What makes a detective mystery?' poster (from Session 1), class story draft, coloured pen (different colour from those used in Session 7).*

*1 See **Revising and editing** on page 7 for more detailed advice.*
2 Redrafting is essential to mystery writing.

- Tell children you are going to revise, edit and improve your class mystery.

- Read the class story or one of the children's stories with the class. Use the 'What makes a detective mystery?' poster to ensure that all elements have been included.

- Ask children to check that the plot makes sense. Do all the suspects have a motive? Is there a final piece of evidence to incriminate the culprit? If the author has just <u>stated</u> that one of the suspects is guilty, further evidence must be provided.

- Look at the vocabulary. Is there a mysterious atmosphere and a build-up of suspense? If not, how could these be included?

- Have flashbacks been included? How could they be improved?

- Is the title appropriate? Does it make the mystery sound exciting?

- Rewrite any sections which require improvement, asking children for suggestions.

Group follow-up activities

red/blue/yellow

Children work on revising and editing their stories in pairs, using the 'What makes a detective mystery?' poster as a reminder of the key elements.

Guided group support

Red Ensure that the plot makes sense and the story has a beginning, middle and end.

Blue Ensure that the plot makes sense and flashbacks are included.

Yellow Help children improve vocabulary to create an atmosphere of suspense.

Plenary Children feed back on their revising and editing work, sharing what they have changed, and discussing how this has improved their stories.

9 Publishing the story

Objectives To understand that there are different ways of publishing a story

To think creatively about different ways of presenting text

To produce a completed book

Shared session *You need: a range of mystery books, revised class story draft, a large sheet of paper, coloured pens.*

*See **Publishing** on page 8 for more detailed notes on the issues involved in the final presentation of the text.*

- Tell children that they are going to decide how to publish the class story.

- Look at a variety of mystery books. Ask children to share ideas about the way they are presented. Look at front and back covers. Are children attracted?

- Ask them to suggest some key things a cover has to do to be successful (e.g. attract the reader's attention, suggest what kind of book/story it is, make the reader curious).

- Look at special illustrations or unusual presentation (e.g. in *Fishing for Clues*, the final chapter, where the murderer is revealed, is kept in a sealed packet at the back). Encourage children to think of other ideas.

■ Decide how many pages you will need. Draw boxes to represent each page on one large sheet of paper. Mark which section of the story is going to be on each page. Plan the layout and make notes about illustrations.

■ Design an eye-catching front cover and write a back-cover blurb.

Group follow-up activities   **red/blue/yellow**

Children work on publishing their own stories.

Guided group support

Red Help children to split the story into reasonable page sections and plan illustrations to match the text.

Blue Encourage children to write an exciting blurb and plan more unusual illustrations to match the text.

Yellow Encourage children to use adventurous illustrations and imaginative text layouts.

Plenary   Children read or present their completed books to the audience.

ADDITIONAL SESSION

How to write a parody of a classic poem

Objectives   To understand the meaning of parody

To write a parody of a classic poem

To experiment with language for humorous effect

Shared session   *You need: OHT/poster 16, a large sheet of paper, coloured pens, paper to mask text.*

*Whilst the classic poem parodied in these notes is **The Charge of the Light Brigade**, any poems that children know well may be used (e.g. **The Highwayman** by Alfred Noyes, **The Listeners** by Walter de la Mare, **Windy Nights** by Robert Louis Stevenson).*

■ Tell children that they are going to learn how to write a **parody** – a version of a story or poem in which some features of the author's writing are changed for comic effect.

■ Identify the intended audience for your poem.

■ Display OHT/poster 16, keeping 'The Charge of the Mouse Brigade' covered. Briefly explain that 'The Charge of the Light Brigade' (first published in 1854) tells the story of the Battle of Balaclava in the Crimean War. Due to someone's blunder, soldiers were sent to fight in a valley where they had no chance of defending themselves. They were attacked by Russian soldiers and hundreds were killed.

■ Read the poem and ask the children to identify and underline the following features:
  ○ repetition (*half a league, cannon, into, rode the six hundred, valley of Death*);
  ○ rhyme scheme (verse 1 – A B C B D B C B).

■ Discuss the effect of these features on the reader. Ask how the writer wanted us to feel about the Light Brigade (that they were brave and heroic in the face of terrible danger).

- Uncover and read 'The Charge of the Mouse Brigade'. Discuss similarities to and differences from the original:

  Similarities
  - Both describe a battle.
  - Some of the original phrases have been retained (*half an ..., into ... valley, rode the six hundred ...*).
  - Line structures and rhythm mimic the original poem. (Demonstrate this by reading small sections of each poem one after the other and clapping the rhythm.)
  - The rhyme scheme is similar to the original but not exactly the same.

  Differences
  - The parody has been made humorous by replacing soldiers with mice and making the objective the 'capture' of some cheese.
  - The verse length and layout are different. Stress that parody does not have to follow the original exactly, as long as the overall effect is recognisable.

- Make a 'How to write a parody' poster to summarise the key points, ensuring that children understand the importance of retaining recognisable features of the original.

- Re-read the second verse, encouraging children to join in. Tell them that you are going to parody this section of the poem together and discuss how to begin. Cannons surround the soldiers; what might be surrounding the mice? Start to write the next verse together on the OHT/poster, discussing rhymes, rhythm and humour.

- Revise and edit your draft.

- Read the final version aloud and tell children they are now going to continue it, working in groups or pairs. Leave the OHT/poster on display for reference.

Group follow-up activities

1 red   **pupil's book page 40**   **copymaster 12**

Using the writing frame on copymaster 12, children continue the parody of 'The Charge of the Light Brigade' by adding another verse.

Guided group support Encourage children to retain some of the original words of the poem, changing others for humorous effect. Help children to maintain a sense of the original rhythm. If necessary, re-read or play an audio-tape of the original poem.

2 blue   **pupil's book page 41**

Children continue the parody of 'The Charge of the Light Brigade'.

Guided group support As for the red group, challenging them to experiment with language.

3 yellow   **pupil's book page 41**

As for the blue group, but using both extracts from 'The Charge of the Light Brigade'.

Guided group support Encourage the children to extend the poem beyond the numbers of verses shown or to choose different subject matter for the parody.

Plenary   Return to the 'How to write a parody' poster. Ask children to contribute ideas based on their experience of writing a parody. Ask for volunteers to share their parodies with the class. Set 'listening targets' (e.g. Is the original recognisable? Is the parody funny? Which lines are particularly effective and why? Could any improvements be made?).

Homework suggestions

- Use a book you have read to identify the features of a detective mystery. **(After Session 1)**
- Use the story of a TV programme to identify the features of a detective mystery. **(After Session 1)**
- Use books you have read to investigate different ways of presenting flashbacks. **(After Session 2)**
- Write an autobiographical flashback, using one of the methods you learnt in class. **(After Session 2)**

- Use books you have read to collect 'mysterious' vocabulary. **(After Session 3)**
- Choose a setting (e.g. home, school, park) and write a mysterious description of it. **(After Session 3)**
- Find books with interesting layouts/front covers, etc. Bring them into school to use for ideas when publishing your own books. **(After Session 8)**

UNIT 3 — How to write a mystery story with flashbacks

Colour the right number of stars to show how well you did the following things:

0 stars = I didn't do it.
1 star = I gave it a try.
2 stars = I did it quite well.

3 stars = I did it well.
4 stars = I did an excellent job!

I planned a detective mystery.	☆	☆	☆	☆
I wrote a plot that made sense.	☆	☆	☆	☆
I described each character's motives.	☆	☆	☆	☆
I included lots of clues.	☆	☆	☆	☆
I built up suspense in my story by using mystery words.	☆	☆	☆	☆
I used flashbacks in my story.	☆	☆	☆	☆
I revealed the final piece of evidence.	☆	☆	☆	☆
I included a 'red herring'.	☆	☆	☆	☆
I improved my story by revising it.	☆	☆	☆	☆

Something I am especially pleased with

Something my audience liked in my writing

Something I'd like to do better next time

Term two non-fiction focus:
4 How to write a balanced report

What most children will already know:

How to write a persuasive text
How to use persuasive language and devices
How to construct a basic argument orally and in writing
How to write in paragraphs

What children will learn in this unit:

To write a report on a controversial issue from both points of view
To organise a balanced report
To use connectives effectively when structuring an argument
To develop the oral and written presentation of an argument
To manipulate an argument to take into account the views of the audience

1 How to organise a balanced report

Objectives
To learn the layout of a balanced report
To understand the purpose of each section of the writing

Shared session
You need: OHTs/posters 17 and 18, paper to mask text, at least 3 different coloured pens, large sheet of paper.

*You may wish to base Session 3 onwards on a controversial subject which is specifically relevant to your class. See note on page 76 and **Homework suggestions** on page 85.*

■ Tell children that they are going to learn how to write a **balanced report** on a controversial issue (an issue that has two opposing points of view). A balanced report presents both sides of the argument fairly.

■ Ask children what the purpose of writing a balanced report might be (to allow the reader to make up their own mind up about an issue).

■ Discuss the differences between a balanced report and a persuasive text (revise children's knowledge of these text types).

> A **persuasive text**:
> strongly supports one point of view;
> selects arguments to support one point of view;
> acknowledges other opinions, but may not give all the evidence needed to support them.
> A **balanced report**:
> looks at both sides equally;
> includes all arguments.

■ Display and read the title only on OHT/poster 17 (mask the rest of the text with a sheet of paper). Ask children what they think the report is about (whale hunting) and who might be on each side of the argument. Can they suggest some arguments that each side might put forward?

■ Uncover and read paragraph 1 and discuss its content and purpose (it summarises the issue, introducing the two opposing viewpoints). Discuss the meaning of the word **summary** (a brief outline with no details). Draw a box around paragraph 1 and label it 'Introduction (summary of issue)'.

- Display and read paragraph 2 and paragraphs 3 and 4 on OHT/poster 18. Using a second colour, draw boxes around these paragraphs. Explain that this is the main part of the report – each paragraph deals with a separate section of the argument. Discuss the main issue in each paragraph and label, for example: paragraph 2 – endangered species; paragraph 3 – traditions; paragraph 4 – methods of killing.

- Re-read paragraph 2. Discuss the fact that within the paragraph, two opposing points of view are being expressed (an **argument** and a **counter-argument**). Using two different colours, underline the arguments 'for' and 'against' whaling. Note that each argument and counter-argument is structured as a point with supporting evidence. Repeat for paragraphs 3 and 4.

- Finally, display and read the final paragraph and discuss its content and purpose. The author concludes the discussion with an analysis of the strengths and weaknesses of the arguments on both sides and a final concluding statement (usually stating a preference or making a recommendation). Using a third colour, draw a box around the final paragraph and label it 'Conclusion (strengths and weaknesses)'.

- Ask children if they think that the writing succeeds in its purpose to put forward a balanced view of the issue.

Group follow-up activities

1 red   copymaster 13

Children read the balanced report on fox hunting and identify the arguments 'for' and 'against' the issue. They then identify the main subject of each paragraph and label the paragraphs accordingly.

Guided group support Help children to identify the main point in each paragraph and to understand that there are 'for' and 'against' opinions in each section.

2 blue   pupil's book page 42   copymaster 14

Children reorganise the mixed-up middle section of a balanced report. (Suggested answer: paragraph 1: 'for' a, 'against' g; paragraph 2: 'for' c, 'against' e; paragraph 3: 'for' d, 'against' h; paragraph 4: 'for' f, 'against' b.) They then write a conclusion.

Guided group support Help children to identify arguments 'for' and 'against' and to organise them into paragraphs. Help them to identify the strongest and weakest arguments on each side.

3 yellow   pupil's book page 43

Children read the middle section of a biased report. They use the box on the left of the page to rewrite the piece as a balanced report, adding their own introduction and conclusion.

Guided group support Encourage children to identify the evidence against fox hunting and to organise it into appropriate paragraphs. Help them to identify the strengths and weaknesses of each argument and to write an introduction and concluding paragraph.

You may wish to ask children to identify the main subject of each paragraph and to label them accordingly, as in the red group activity.

Plenary

Make a class poster entitled 'How to write a balanced report'. Ask children what they have learnt about organising a balanced report and write their responses on the poster. (Keep the poster as you will be adding to it in subsequent sessions.) Reinforce the key points of the teaching session (differences between a balanced report and a persuasive text; basic structure of a balanced report – summary, main body (presenting both sides fairly), concluding analysis).

② Investigating the style and language of a balanced report

Objectives   To understand the stylistic features of a balanced report

To collect words and phrases which will be useful when writing a balanced report

Shared session   *You need: OHTs/posters 17 and 18, 'How to write a balanced report' poster (from Session 1), copymaster 15, large sheet of paper, coloured pens.*

- Tell children that they are going to find out about the style of a balanced report and collect some words and phrases that will be useful when writing their own report.

- Re-read the report on OHTs/posters 17 and 18. Ask children to identify the tense of the writing (present tense). Underline the present tense verbs to reinforce this point (e.g. *is, argue, believe, are*).

- Note that the writing is impersonal – there is no use of *I* or *we*. The two sides involved in the debate are identified (underline *whaling nations, anti-whaling countries*) and the pronoun *they* is used. Discuss why the writing is impersonal (the argument is supposed to be balanced, so any use of personal pronouns would signal the author's point of view, thus biasing the text).

- Discuss the use of technical vocabulary. Underline some examples (e.g. *commercial whaling, extinction, endangered*) and discuss their meanings. Remind the children that points must always be backed up by evidence and this sometimes involves using technical vocabulary.

- Look at paragraph 2 of OHT/poster 18. Ask children why the word *butchered* is in quotation marks (it is the actual word that the biologist used). Explain that if they quote other people's words as evidence in their argument, they must put the words in quotation marks and acknowledge the source.

- Ask children to find words and phrases that will be useful when they write their own arguments. List these on a class poster called 'Useful words and phrases'.

- Ask children to pick out the phrases that the author uses when putting forward the different points of view. Underline *argue that, believe that, acknowledge this, dispute this,* etc. Add these to the poster under the heading 'Introducing points of view', putting a line before each one to signal that a name or a pronoun should precede each phrase (e.g. '_____ argue that ...').

- Ask children to identify and underline connectives (e.g. *although, consequently, therefore, while, however*). Explain that these words do different jobs: some help to structure one side of the argument, while others help to introduce the opposite point of view. Return to the text and discuss the job of each connective. List them on the class chart under two headings: 'structuring the argument' (e.g. *therefore, consequently*) and 'opposite views' (e.g. *although, while, however*). As an extension, the children can add other words they know to this list (e.g. *as a result, alternatively, obviously, whereas, nevertheless*).

Group follow-up activities

Texts at the appropriate level will need to be provided for this activity.

1 red   pupil's book page 44

Children use the connective word bank to complete the sentences. They then use other texts to collect different connectives. Alternatively, children could use some of the connectives in their own sentences.

Guided group support Encourage children to put different connectives into the sentences and discuss how this changes the meaning. Ask them to choose the best connective for each sentence.

2 blue   pupil's book page 44   copymaster 15

Note that there is more than one way of completing this exercise.

Children read the balanced report about catching dolphins in tuna nets and use the word banks provided to complete the cloze exercise. As an extension, they may write a concluding paragraph for the piece.

Guided group support Encourage children to experiment with different connectives, noting how they can change the meaning of the sentence. Reinforce the use of impersonal language in the final paragraph.

3 yellow   pupil's book page 45

Children use the information on the tuna debate to write the middle section and concluding paragraph of a balanced report, using the vocabulary and techniques discussed in the shared session.

Guided group support Encourage children to use impersonal language, a range of connectives and a final paragraph which includes some analysis of the strengths and weaknesses of the arguments.

Plenary Ask children what they have learnt about the style of a balanced report. Write their responses on the 'How to write a balanced report' poster from Session 1. Reinforce the main points of the lesson (use of present tense, impersonal language and technical vocabulary, using quotation marks and acknowledging sources). Ask children to contribute any new words they have found to the 'Useful words and phrases' poster you made in the shared session. Ask volunteers from the yellow and blue groups to read their reports. Encourage the rest of the class to identify use of impersonal language, present tense and connectives.

③ How to construct an effective argument

Objectives

To construct an effective argument by organising information

To develop points logically

To support and illustrate points persuasively

To appeal to the known views of the audience

Shared session *You need: children's research, OHT/poster 19, coloured pens, copymaster 17 (enlarged to A3/A2).*

The materials provided relate to homework as a controversial issue. However, you could adapt this session to focus on an issue chosen by the children themselves.
The children will need to have completed some research into the issue before this lesson, either in school or at home (see **Homework suggestions** *on page 85). The notes in italics suggest how writing questionnaires for use in children's research may be modelled in the shared session.*

■ A good way for the children to collect information is by using questionnaires which they have designed themselves. Demonstrate how to construct a questionnaire by initially showing children a variety of printed examples. Look at the different ways in which responses are recorded (e.g. multiple-choice answers, answers which demand a level of agreement with a statement (agree–disagree–don't know), answers which are completed freely by the participant).

■ Decide which kind of responses the children think will be most useful for their research and look at how questions are phrased to elicit these responses. Write some questions with the children to demonstrate this. For example:

Homework helps children to do better at school.
Agree   Disagree   Don't know
What do you think is the most important thing for children to do at home?
Play   Homework
How do you think homework helps children?
Free response

Note that the first example is actually a statement, not a question, and therefore just asks for some level of agreement.

■ After writing their questionnaires the children should decide who will complete them so that their research is balanced, not biased. This research can then be used in the debate and the final written report.

■ Tell children that they are going to hold a debate about the issue of homework (or their chosen issue) and then write a report of the debate. Two opposing sides will argue for and against the motion 'Is homework valuable?'.

■ Explain that they are going to prepare arguments for the debate. Display OHT/poster 19. This is information collected by researchers investigating the value of homework. Remind children that when constructing an argument a **point** must be supported by **evidence**. Explain that the points and evidence 'for' and 'against' homework are mixed up, and need to be sorted out.

■ Display the enlarged copymaster 17. Explain that this is a framework to enable children to put forward their point of view effectively during a debate. Add the heading 'Debate plan'. Work with the children to split the points on OHT/poster 19 into 'for' and 'against' and list them on the framework. Discuss which points are opposite views of the same argument and list these on the chart in note form.

■ Give each argument a title. This helps to reinforce the concept that this is a balanced discussion with points and evidence 'for' and 'against' each argument. Some possible titles for the arguments: 'Parents and children', 'Exam results', 'Use of time'.

■ Return to OHT/poster 19. Discuss which evidence could be used to support each point. Using a different colour, write the evidence onto the chart in note form (e.g. argument – 'Parents and children'; evidence 'for' – improves relationship, parents interested in children's school work, spend time talking, not watching TV; evidence 'against' – causes arguments as parents force children to do homework).

■ Keep the completed chart for use in Session 5.

■ Establish that the audience at the debate will be made up of children, teachers and parents (with the children themselves playing these different roles). At the end of the debate a vote will be taken. The speakers on both sides will have to use persuasive arguments that will win them as many votes as possible. Explain that they will need to consider the possible viewpoints of the different groups in the audience. Discuss who is likely to be in favour and who might be against and how the speakers might use this information to win votes.

■ Recap on children's knowledge of persuasive devices. For example, if the audience is made up of parents, pro-homework debaters might appeal directly to them by using rhetorical questions such as 'Surely you want to be involved in the education of your child?'. Similarly, anti-homework debaters could appeal to them with questions such as 'Surely you don't want your child to be unhappy and under stress about schoolwork?'.

■ Explain to children that if they have considered the arguments that the opposition might put forward, then they can prepare in advance how to counter them (thus strengthening their own argument). It is effective to actually acknowledge the opposing view before putting their case forward (e.g. '<u>Of course</u> some homework activities are valuable, <u>but</u> ...').

■ Now ask children to choose the strongest and weakest arguments against homework, justifying their choices, and to suggest an order for presenting them. Remind them that it is a good idea to begin and end with strong arguments, as these give a first and last impression. Weaker arguments (e.g. opinion disguised as fact) can be better placed in the middle of the piece.

■ Tell children that they are now going to construct an argument about homework in preparation for the debate.

Group follow-up activities

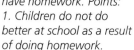

Adapt copymaster 16 by filling in the following opening statement and points for the children. Opening statement: I believe that primary school children should not have homework. Points:
1. Children do not do better at school as a result of doing homework.
2. Children should not be doing extra schoolwork at home. All work should be done in school.
3. Homework can cause arguments between parents and children.

Arguing in favour of homework may be slightly less appealing to children, so you might need to encourage some to prepare the case 'for' homework. You need to ensure that there is an equal number on both sides of the argument.

red 1   pupil's book page 46   copymaster 16

Children work as a group or in pairs. They match evidence in the pupil's book against homework to the points written in on copymaster 16. They use their own research to add a fourth point against homework, and then write a final summary of their position. Each child presents their case to the group, and a volunteer is chosen to present to the whole class in the plenary.

Guided group support Help children to choose the appropriate evidence for the given points. Encourage them to speak confidently to the group.

2 blue/yellow   pupil's book pages 46–47   copymaster 16

Children work as a group or in pairs. They match the evidence to the points and use their own research to construct an extra argument 'for' or 'against' homework. They use copymaster 16 to construct an opening statement declaring their position, decide on the order of the arguments, and summarise their point of view at the end. They then present their case to the group.

Guided group support

Blue Help children to match the appropriate points and evidence, give a final summary of their views and speak confidently to the group. Encourage them to think of possible objections to their arguments and how they might counter them.

Yellow Help children to combine their own research with the information given and to organise it into appropriate categories.

3 yellow   pupil's book page 47

As an extension, children think about possible objections to their arguments and how they might counter them. They then present their case to the group.

Plenary

Ask the children what they have learnt about constructing an argument. Reinforce the main objectives of the lesson by asking volunteers to read their arguments. Ask the class to listen out for the following things:

- Has the speaker included points from their own research?
- Are all the points supported by evidence?
- Is the position of the speaker clear?
- Have the strongest arguments been presented first and last?
- Should the order be rearranged?

4 Holding a debate

Objectives

To present an effective and logical argument

To argue points supported by evidence in a logical way

To understand that there are two sides to a controversial issue

Shared session

You need: a stopwatch or clock, children's debate frameworks from Session 3.

Holding a debate is an important step before writing a balanced report. The children need to verbalise and hear both points of view before attempting to write them down.

- Appoint a chairperson. Explain that it is their job to announce the issue to be debated and control the debate. You may wish to take on this role yourself unless the children are familiar with holding class discussions.

- Divide the children into two groups: 'for' and 'against' (according to the position they took in Session 3). Explain that they will be arguing 'for' or 'against', using their debate frameworks.

There are several different ways of holding a debate, and the event can be as big or as small as you choose. A debate needs seven basic components:

1. A controversial statement on an issue

2. A group to support the statement

3. A group to oppose the statement

4. A chairperson

5. A timekeeper

6. A venue

7. An audience

You can use any room to hold a debate, but the supporters of the issue should sit together, as should the opposition.

You can also hold a school/community debate, keeping the same format but widening the audience to include 'real' representatives of each interested party (e.g. parents, other teachers, headteacher, children from another class). This takes more organisation, but the children can be involved in discussing who to invite, writing and sending invitations, etc.

■ Appoint a timekeeper. Explain that their job is to set a limit on how much time each side has to speak, and enforce it. This allows both sides equal amounts of time to express their views and stops over-zealous speakers monopolising the debate. They will time the speakers using a stopwatch or clock.

■ The other children will be the audience, and will vote on the issue at the end of the debate. If the debate is on homework, some children will need to be in role as teachers, others as parents and some as themselves to make the voting fair (as it is likely that the children themselves would vote against!). This can be difficult for some children, but the use of props such as badges or stickers confirming their new identity can have an amazing effect. If the debate is on another issue, then the audience should include representatives of all interested parties. Children should be allocated roles accordingly. (To avoid repetition of the same points, you could allocate each speaker a specific point to argue.)

■ Before the debate begins give the opposing sides time to designate three main speakers who will use the notes prepared in the previous session to put forward their point of view.

■ Establish rules with the children about how long each person will be allowed to speak. The following is a suggested format for the debate, which will ensure that all children have the opportunity to express their opinions:

1. Chairperson introduces issue
2. Speaker 1 – support
3. Speaker 1 – opposition
4. Speaker 2 – support
5. Speaker 2 – opposition
6. Speaker 3 – support
7. Speaker 3 – opposition
8. Questions from the debating teams
9. Questions from the audience
10. Final vote

Group follow-up activities

red/blue/yellow

Children participate in debate.

Plenary

Evaluate the result of the debate with the children. Did the vote go as expected? Why? Why not?

Which arguments were presented well? Why? Were there any arguments which could have been improved? How? Could this have made a difference to the vote?

⑤ Planning a balanced report

Objectives

To plan a balanced report in note form

To select relevant information

To organise arguments

Shared session

You need: 'How to write a balanced report' poster (from Session 1), 'Debate plan' (from Session 3), OHT/poster 20.

■ Tell children that they are now going to write a balanced report about the issue debated in the previous session (this could be a report of the actual debate). First, establish a real purpose and audience for the report (e.g. an article for the school magazine, a leaflet to be distributed in school or put in the school library).

- Tell children that they are going to plan the report first in note form. Display OHT/poster 20. Reinforce the difference between a balanced report and a persuasive argument (a balanced report should present both sides of the issue equally).

- Can children think of a 'catchy' title that will make people want to read the report? Remind them that the title should inform the reader about the issue that is going to be discussed.

- Recap on what the first paragraph should contain (a summary of the issue), and write planning notes in the box, for example:

  > SUMMARY OF ISSUE
  > Details of debate (if appropriate) – where, when, who spoke for each side
  > Homework very important – educational
  > Homework unnecessary burden on children

Possible titles for the arguments are: 'Results', 'Parents and children', 'Use of time', 'Life skills'.
If you are writing a report of the debate itself then model how to refer to the speakers (e.g. 'Tom stressed that ..., but Sarah argued in response that ...').

- Recap on the main arguments from the debate (you could refer back to the debate plan from Session 3). Decide on a title for each argument, and stress that each one will be contained within its own paragraph. Write notes for the points and evidence 'for' and 'against' each argument as they were presented in the debate.

- Plan the concluding paragraph. This demands analysis of the arguments. Ask children to identify the strongest and weakest arguments 'for' and 'against' and to justify their choice. Write this up in note form in the box for the final paragraph, for example:

  > 'For':   strongest – improved exam results – research from OFSTED
  > weakest – improves parent/child relationship – no proof – varies between families

- Keep the completed plan for use in Session 6.

- Tell children that they are now going to plan their own reports in note form. Make sure that they understand that they will have to select the most important points from the mass of information gathered during the debate.

Group follow-up activities

Scaffolding can be provided by cutting down the number of arguments in the middle section; providing the argument headings; giving the points and asking children to fill in the evidence; planning the opening paragraph; planning the argument as a group.

red copymaster 17

Children use their research and information from Sessions 3 and 4 to plan a balanced report.

Guided group support Help children to organise the information into relevant paragraphs and to write in note form when planning. Encourage them to include at least two arguments in the middle section.

blue copymaster 17

Children use their research and information from Sessions 3 and 4 to plan a balanced report.

Guided group support As for the red group. Also, encourage children to include at least three arguments in the middle section.

yellow copymaster 17

Children use their research and information from Sessions 3 and 4 to plan a balanced report.

Guided group support As for the red and blue groups, but encourage children to include at least four arguments in the middle section and to analyse their strengths and weaknesses in the final paragraph.

Plenary Ask children what they have learnt about planning a balanced report. Address any problems that they have experienced at the planning stage (e.g. using full sentences instead of notes, organising points, matching evidence to points, analysing strengths and weaknesses). Use a volunteer's plans to demonstrate how the problems might be solved.

6 Drafting the balanced report

Objectives To write a balanced report, following a plan

To include words and phrases which structure arguments and develop opposing arguments

To analyse strengths and weaknesses of opposing arguments

Shared session *You need: 'How to write a balanced report' poster (from Session 1), 'Useful words and phrases' poster (from Session 2), OHT/poster 20 (from Session 5), large sheets of paper, coloured pens.*

*See **Drafting** on page 7 for more detailed advice on conducting a whole-class drafting session.*

■ Tell children that you are going to draft a balanced class report. Display the class poster 'How to write a balanced report' and the 'Useful words and phrases' poster alongside the plan on OHT/poster 20 as you write. Remind children about the different uses of connectives, referring to the posters.

■ Write the report with the children, constantly re-reading to check that the writing makes sense. You will need to remain in firm control of the writing, whilst asking children for their contributions.

■ Reinforce the concept that the writing should be impersonal. Make explicit references to connectives and argumentative words and phrases throughout the writing.

■ Different colours can be used for different sections of the writing to emphasise the structure.

■ Read the completed report through with the children. Remind them that this is only a first draft and that further modifications may be needed at the redrafting stage.

■ Tell children that they are now going to draft their own reports.

Group follow-up activities **red/blue/yellow**

Children draft their reports, following their plans.

Guided group support

Red Help children to follow their plan when writing and to use a variety of connectives.

Blue Help children to follow their writing plan, using appropriate connectives and a variety of ways of introducing different points of view.

Yellow Encourage children to use a variety of connectives and ways of introducing different points of view. Help them to write a final paragraph which effectively analyses the strengths and weaknesses of the different positions.

For the red group, further support may be given by drafting the first paragraph together; having the first and final paragraphs already written so that children can concentrate on the middle section of the report; providing the first sentence of each paragraph.

Plenary Ask children if they experienced any difficulties when drafting the report, or address any points which have arisen during the shared session. Reflect on these difficulties and revise key points (e.g. using impersonal language, analysing strengths and weaknesses of arguments, using connectives appropriately, introducing different points of view in a variety of ways).

7 Revising and editing the balanced report

Objectives To assess the effectiveness of the report

To improve the report by revising and editing

Shared session *You need: 'How to write a balanced report' poster (from Session 1), 'Useful words and phrases' poster (from Session 2), OHT/poster 20 (from Session 5), coloured pen (different colour from those used in Session 6), class report draft.*

 See Revising and editing on page 7 for more detailed advice.

■ Tell children that you are going to revise and edit the class report you began in the previous session.

■ Read through your draft. Ask children how well the report introduces the issue, presents both points of view and sums up. Encourage them to identify points which they think could be improved. (Use these as revision focuses.)

You will need to assign a revision focus to each child and write it on their work. You may wish to correct other errors which are not part of the revision focus, or spend another session proofreading for spelling and punctuation errors.

■ Choose one or more of the following revision focuses: organisation of arguments, evidence to support points, balance within the report, impersonal language, use of connectives, effective summary of arguments, effective analysis of strengths and weaknesses of arguments. Choose your revision focus on the basis of any difficulties which may have arisen in plenary sessions or when marking the draft arguments. Write the revision focus at the top of a sheet of paper.

■ Discuss possible changes and improvements with the children and alter the text accordingly (using a different colour).

■ Tell children that they are going to revise and edit their own reports.

Group follow-up activities **red/blue/yellow**

Children work on revising and editing their reports.

Guided group support

Red Help children to check that their arguments make sense and that they have put forward both sides of the argument.

Blue Help children to check that both sides of one argument are put forward in the same paragraph and that connectives are used appropriately.

Yellow Encourage children to examine the final paragraph and check that the strengths and weaknesses of both sides have been analysed. Ensure that connectives have been used appropriately.

Plenary Children feed back on their revising and editing work. They report on what they have learnt and how this will help them when they write arguments in the future. Ask children to give examples of something they changed, and describe how this improved their writing in relation to their revision focus.

8 Publishing the balanced report

Objective To present a balanced report

Shared session *You need: revised class report draft, examples of balanced reports from magazines/newspapers, OHTs/posters 17 and 18, large sheet of paper, coloured pens.*

*1 See **Publishing** on page 8 for more detailed notes on the issues involved in the final presentation of the text.*
*2 You may wish to ask children to collect some newspaper/ magazine articles as a homework task (see **Homework suggestions**, page 85).*

■ Tell children that you are going to publish your class report. Remind them of the purpose of the writing and discuss methods of presentation as a magazine or newspaper article.

■ Display some newspaper/magazine articles and/or OHTs/posters 17 and 18. Analyse the layout of the articles and the different fonts and text sizes used. The title will normally have a larger text size and maybe a different font in order to make it stand out. Discuss if there is any other part of the article which stands out. On OHT/poster 17 a larger text size is used for the summary in the first paragraph. Discuss the reasons for this.

■ Look at any illustrations/photographs. Discuss why illustrations/photographs supporting both sides of the argument must be presented in order for the piece to remain balanced. Use the photographs on OHTs/posters 17 and 18 to demonstrate this.

■ Using a large piece of paper, plan the layout. Use different coloured pens for each section. Add notes to show where each part of the writing will be located, and the fonts and sizes to be used. If illustrations are to be included, draw boxes to show where they are to be placed, and write notes about the picture in each box.

■ Tell the children that they are going to draw a plan and publish their own reports.

Group follow-up activities

red/blue/yellow

Children present their reports.

Guided group support

Red Support may be given by planning the report as a group, or offering a list of illustration ideas for the children to choose from. Encourage children to change text size for effect and to include two illustrations to reflect both sides of the argument.

Blue As for the red group. Also, encourage children to use different text sizes and fonts where appropriate.

Yellow As for the red and blue groups. Also, encourage children to write appropriate captions for their chosen illustrations, avoiding bias.

Plenary Ask children to share some of their reports and discuss the most effective use of fonts, illustrations, etc. The reports could then be presented to the intended audience (e.g. you could publish the class report in the school magazine or distribute children's work to other classes and/or parents as information leaflets).

ADDITIONAL SESSION

Using 'official' language

Objectives   To understand that there is a difference between 'official' and 'everyday' language

To understand the contexts in which official language might be used

Shared session   *You need: OHTs/posters 21 and 22, large piece of paper, coloured pens.*

Before this lesson, homework could be set, asking children to collect some examples of 'official' language (see **Homework suggestions** *on page 85).*

■ Ask children to describe what they think 'official' language is and to share examples that they have collected.

■ Clarify the meaning of 'official' language by explaining that it is language used in important documents, which has to be formal and precise to ensure that its meaning is clear to everyone who reads it, thus avoiding misunderstandings. It is used in important and official legal documents (such as guarantees, financial documents, passports, etc.) as it is very important that documents like these are clear and easy to understand by everyone who reads them.

■ Display OHT/poster 21. Ask children to pick out the 'official' words: *admittance, trespassers, prosecuted, prohibited*. Discuss their meanings and why they have been used on signs. Point out that the instructions on the signs are enforceable by law. Reinforce the point that official language is universal, and its meaning is clear to everyone. Illustrate this by rewriting one of the signs using dialect or slang (e.g. 'Anyone who comes in here will be nicked') and discussing possible different interpretations of this.

■ Display OHT/poster 22 and explain that this is a holiday booking form. Discuss the reasons why this form needed to be written using official language (it establishes an official agreement between the customer and the travel agent, it is a legally binding document, it records financial information).

■ Work with the children to underline the 'official' vocabulary on the booking form. Some of the terms used may be unfamiliar to the children and will need to be explained (e.g. *deposit, correspondence, to whom*). Discuss why *Date of Birth* is used instead of *Birthday*. (*Birthday* implies that only a date is required (e.g. 16th August), whereas *Date of Birth* means that the year must also be written, for example 16th August 1968.)

■ Note the use of present tense (e.g. *I enclose deposits*) and passive verbs (e.g. *correspondence should be sent*). Explain that these language features are typical of the official style. Ask children if they can remember any other features of formal language (e.g. using nouns instead of verbs (*no admittance* instead of *no one can enter*), and impersonal language. However, note that the booking form is a personal customer agreement, therefore it addresses the customer directly as *you*.

■ Explain to children that they are going to design their own booking form. Establish a purpose and audience for their writing, for example a booking form for a school trip (for parents) or an application form for an after school or lunchtime club (for pupils).

■ Make a poster, entitled 'How to write an official form'. List the information that is requested on the form (title of tour/holiday, name, flight details, insurance, hotel, travel agent, credit card details). Discuss with the children what information from the class poster will be useful when designing their form. Children may not require all this information for their writing, but it provides a bank which they can choose from. You could underline the terms which you think will be useful for the children's own writing.

Further sessions could be used to revise, edit and present the forms. Children could also design their forms on computers.

■ Look at the layout of the form. Discuss whether the form is easy to fill in and why (the information required is laid out in clear sections in boxes, with enough space to write in). You may wish to design part of the form together with the children before they tackle this as a group task.

Group follow-up activities

1 red/blue/yellow   pupil's book page 48

Children use the class poster to help them to design a form for a specific purpose. They then swap forms with their partners and complete each other's. This highlights any unsatisfactory layout or wording of the form and enables real revising and editing to take place.

Guided group support

Red Scaffolding may be provided by giving the children a frame containing some key words and phrases (e.g. 'Trip title'; 'Surname'; 'Do you require coach travel? If not, please state your method of transport'; 'Activities'). Encourage children to use some official language when writing their form.

Blue/Yellow Help children to make the layout clear and to use appropriate official language.

2 red/blue/yellow   pupil's book page 49

As an additional activity, children translate some signs written in 'official' language into everyday language. As a further extension, children could write some signs for use in the classroom (e.g. 'Library books must be returned promptly after use').

Plenary Ask what children have learnt about using official language. Discuss any problems/difficulties which occurred when writing their forms. Ask the children to share some of their forms. Discuss the clarity of the forms and whether 'official' language has been used appropriately.

Homework suggestions

Encourage children to note their sources, organise their information and write any direct quotations they think will be useful in quotation marks.

○ Find as much factual information as you can about your chosen subject. You can use library books, magazines and the internet; carry out surveys and interviews with your family and friends; write to different organisations to ask for information. **(Before Session 3)**

○ Look for balanced reports in newspapers, magazines, leaflets, etc. and bring them into school. Investigate the written structure, or note the points made and the evidence used to support them. **(After Session 1)**

○ Note examples of balanced reporting in TV and radio news programmes. **(After Session 1)**

○ Look for examples of connectives in balanced reports from newspapers and magazines. Make a list of words to add to the 'Useful words and phrases' chart. **(After Session 2)**

○ Look for different ways of presenting points of view in newspapers and magazines. Make a list to add to the 'Useful words and phrases' chart. **(After Session 3)**

○ Look at the presentation and layout of balanced reports in newspapers/magazines. **(After Session 7)**

○ Look at how photographs and illustrations are used in reports. Is the presentation biased or balanced? **(After Session 7)**

○ Collect some examples of 'official' language. Look on signs, information leaflets, instructions or guarantees for games or other products. **(After Session 8)**

UNIT 4 How to write a balanced report

Colour the right number of stars to show how well you did the following things:

0 stars = I didn't do it.   3 stars = I did it well.
1 star = I gave it a try.   4 stars = I did an excellent job!
2 stars = I did it quite well.

I summarised the issue.	☆	☆	☆	☆
I reported both sides of the issue equally.	☆	☆	☆	☆
I constructed good arguments.	☆	☆	☆	☆
I used evidence to support my points.	☆	☆	☆	☆
I used connectives to develop my arguments.	☆	☆	☆	☆
I used quotations and acknowledged the source.	☆	☆	☆	☆
I used impersonal language.	☆	☆	☆	☆
My conclusion analysed the strengths and weaknesses of both sides of the argument.	☆	☆	☆	☆

Something I am especially pleased with

Something my audience liked in my writing

Something I'd like to do better next time

Term three fiction focus:
5 How to write a book review

1 Identifying the key features of a book review

Objective To identify the key structural and linguistic features of a book review

Shared session *You need: OHTs/posters 23 and 24, large sheet of paper, coloured pens, paper to mask text.*

It is likely that many children will have read independently some or all of the Harry Potter books. However, for the purposes of this session, you may want to share some excerpts of text from **Harry Potter and the Philosopher's Stone** *with the whole class beforehand.*

■ Tell the children that over the next few sessions they are going to learn how to write a book review.

■ Ask what kind of information they would expect to find in a book review (e.g. reviewer's opinions about the characters, setting, plot, language/style and usually a recommendation (either positive or negative) to potential readers).

■ Ask why people might want to read reviews (e.g. to decide whether they might want to read the book themselves for pleasure; to find out how useful a book might be for a specific purpose such as study/research; to help them choose books for other people to read, in the case of librarians, booksellers or teachers).

■ Ask the children if they themselves have ever chosen a book as a result of reading a review of it. Tell them they are going to read a review of a Harry Potter book, and briefly discuss how and why the series became so popular so quickly. Ask how they first heard about the books – did someone recommend them, did they see an advert or read a review?

■ Brainstorm key facts about the characters, setting and plot of the first book and write them up, noting also the children's opinions about them. Ask children for their views on a few other points such as favourite moments, any weaknesses and the effectiveness of the ending.

■ Display and read OHTs/posters 23 and 24, masking the final paragraph. Ask children to think about who might have written the review and its likely purpose and audience (style and register indicate that this is probably a child writing for others of a similar age to inform them about the book).

■ Ask if they think the reviewer liked the book and how they might end the text (e.g. with a conclusion in which they recommend the book). Read the final paragraph to check.

- Focus on the structure of the review, asking the children to identify and label the following sections. Discuss the content and function of each section with the class:

Title:	eye-catching
	acts like a newspaper headline to make people want to read the review
Introduction:	needs to be lively to get the reader interested and make them want to read on
	contains brief descriptions about the characters, setting and plot
	gives reader a feel of what the book is about
Commentary:	different paragraphs containing more detailed information (usually focusing on character, setting, plot, style/language, audience)
Recommendation:	gives a recommendation; often mentions target readers

- Note that details about the book are given below the title, and ask why (so that people can ask for the book in a bookshop if the review made them want to buy it).

- Focus on the language of the review, asking the children to identify and underline examples of the following:

  - style – is it formal or informal? (informal, for example *Harry makes lots of great magic friends at Hogwarts; they're great fun, and always up to crazy tricks*)

  - verbs – mainly active forms, in the present tense. Note that although the past tense is usually used for narrative, the present tense is used when summarising the plot of a story

  - connectives to show the sequence of events (e.g. <u>When</u> *he is just a baby; up to the age of …*)

  - connectives to show contrasting views (e.g. <u>Although</u> *the suspense is carefully built, there is one problem …; … just too hard to believe in.* <u>However,</u> *…*).

- Ask why discursive language is common in this type of text (because a review often balances positive and negative comments).

- Ask the children to look for phrases that they think might be used in reviews of any good book (e.g. *The story keeps us on the edge of our seats; readers who enjoy … should appreciate …*).

Group follow-up activities

1 red/blue/yellow   pupil's book pages 50–51

Children read the introductory section of another Harry Potter book review. They make notes on the information it contains, using a given framework.

Guided group support Discuss with the children the amount and type of detail necessary to include in an introduction.

2 blue/yellow   pupil's book page 52

Children go on to read the commentary section of the review. In pairs, or as a group, they analyse the balance of negative and positive opinions and predict what kind of recommendation the writer might make. You might want them to list these in their books, or to use an acetate sheet to mark them.

Guided group support Direct children towards the words in the text that offer or imply an opinion – for example, words with positive connotations. Use these as a basis for speculating what the author might have added as a recommendation about the book.

3 yellow   pupil's book page 52

As an extension, children write the recommendation, in pairs or as a group.

Guided group support Encourage children to consider how to take negative points into account and balance them against positive points when writing a recommendation.

Plenary

Begin to compile a class poster entitled 'A successful book review should include …'. Ask children what they have learnt about the structure and content of a book review, and write up their comments under the following headings: 'Introduction', 'Commentary', 'Recommendation'.

Ask the blue group to report some of the criticisms in the commentary they looked at and the yellow group to offer some positive points. Discuss briefly why reviews often point out weaknesses as well as strengths (to give a fair and honest assessment). If there is time, invite volunteers from the yellow group to read out their recommendations, and discuss any differences between them. Here is the actual recommendation that concluded the review:

> 'However, after a slow start, *Harry Potter and the Goblet of Fire* really begins to sparkle half way through with Rowling's familiar magic … This book is pivotal, not just for the author, for whom the heat is well and truly on, but for Harry and his readers who, by the last chapter, are left in little doubt that there is much more to come. (Age 10 to adult.)'

② Planning a book review

Objectives

To create a planning framework for a book review for a particular audience and purpose

To make effective planning notes (drawing upon reading journal notes, as appropriate)

To brainstorm, prioritise and select information

To make preliminary decisions about how to sequence and present key pieces of information

Shared session

You need: large sheet of paper, coloured pens, 'A successful book review should include …' poster (from Session 1).

*1 See **Planning** on page 6 for further guidance on planning a shared text.*

*2 If children have been keeping reading journals for some time prior to this writing project, all the necessary information and opinions should already be recorded and should only need reorganising into the planning framework. You may wish to allow the children a short time prior to this session to refer to their journal entries in preparation for the class discussion, and also to have them to hand for reference during the discussion. See the additional session **Keeping a reading journal** on page 94.*

- Explain to children that they are going to produce a review collection, featuring a class review (which you will write together) and individual reviews of books of their choice. The purpose will be to help potential readers to choose a book that they might enjoy. So, although negative points can be included, each review should be balanced overall. You could also choose a different purpose for the work (e.g. 'top ten' favourite books, recommended books for particular age groups. See **Homework suggestions** on page 103 for other ideas).

- Discuss how you might publish and circulate the collection (e.g. by placing copies in the school library and giving them to other classes). You might want to consider submitting reviews for publication on a book website.

- Decide upon the book to be reviewed by the whole class. Preferably, it should be the text which the class read together most recently. Decide on your target audience. At this point you may also wish to decide what books the pupils will go on to review independently (if appropriate, with reference to the children's reading journals). Some children may find it difficult to make their choice, so establish a time and place for them to come and seek help with this. Establish also whether children can choose to work with a partner.

■ Ask the children to brainstorm key information about the book's plot, characters and setting (use these as headings to organise the notes you take). Who are the main characters? What is the main situation/problem? What are the key events? Where do they take place?

■ On a large sheet of paper, draw up a framework for the review. Ask the children to name the main sections (introduction, commentary, recommendation) and recap on what they should contain.

■ Ask children to brainstorm notes for the introduction, which should include vital, but brief, details explaining what the book is about (e.g. main situation, characters).

You may want to take a quick class vote on any contentious points, so that you are working with the majority view.

■ Explain that you will plan the recommendation section first of all – it is important to decide whether or not you are going to make a positive recommendation before you start to write, as this will affect what you decide to say in the commentary section. For example, it would be odd to make lots of criticisms in the commentary, and then to recommend the book strongly. Ask for children's general opinions on the book. Did they enjoy it, would they recommend it and to whom? Identify the book's genre and decide upon a target readership. What key adjectives might sum up the book's appeal? Note all the points on the framework.

■ Now focus on planning the commentary section. Elicit paragraph headings from the children (e.g. plot, characterisation, setting, the writer's comic or inventive style). The sequence of paragraphs will depend upon what you agree to be the key aspects of the book (e.g. if the setting is very important then you might comment on that first). Are there any weaknesses to note down too? Taking each heading in turn, make brief notes of children's opinions on your framework. Encourage children to give reasons and evidence from the text.

■ If children have read other books by the same author and/or on the same subject, mention these in the review and compare them with the present text.

■ Tell children that they are now going to plan their own book reviews.

Group follow-up activities

1 red/blue/yellow   pupil's book page 53

Children plan their own book reviews. They brainstorm key information for each section, with help from prompts in the pupil's book, and then plan the introduction, commentary and recommendation accordingly.

Guided group support

Red Ensure that children are clear on what they want to say about their chosen book. Help them to brainstorm and make notes. Ensure they are able to create a suitable structure for presenting their points, using helpful sub-headings. If necessary, allow them to use the framework from the class review for their note-making.

Blue Encourage children to balance their enthusiasm with some realistic criticisms of the text.

Yellow As for the blue group. Also, challenge this group to try to see the text through the eyes of other readers as well as from their own point of view.

Plenary

Invite volunteers to give a brief summary of their chosen book (referring to their planning notes as a prompt if necessary). Ask them to explain how they will structure their commentary section and why.

3 Drafting the book review

Objectives

To compile a text, guided by a plan

To compose a range of sentence types

To select and use language for specific effects

Shared session

You need: planning framework (from Session 2), OHTs/posters 23 and 24, large sheet of paper, coloured pens.

*1 See **Drafting** on page 7 for more detailed advice on conducting a whole-class drafting session.*

*2 There is a great deal involved in writing a book review. You may wish to spread the following work over two sessions. To help you plan this, the notes have been divided into three sections: **Introduction**, **Commentary** and **Recommendation**.*

■ Tell children that you are going to use the planning framework you made in Session 2 to draft your class book review.

■ Remind children of the purpose of writing (to give a clear, fair and balanced impression of what the book is like to potential readers) and of your target audience. Display the planning framework.

Introduction

■ Recap that the introduction needs to give the reader a feel for what the book is actually about. It should include vital details about plot, character and setting. Look in more detail at the introductory paragraph on OHT/poster 23. Recap the important language features used (present tense, active verbs). Look at how the first sentences sum up the opening situation/event using lively, interesting language, and introduce the main characters. The paragraph continues with a sequence of key events, which are described briefly. Discuss where and how important details and names are woven in. The writing is as concise as possible.

■ Now draft the introduction for the class review, referring to your planning framework. Draft the opening sentences and then work through the sequence of key events. Discuss how to describe things in as few words as possible. Refer back to your planning notes as you work, checking with the children which of the important characters and details have been included, and looking at how relatively important they are (is the emphasis right?). Model how to weave the characters into the draft.

Commentary

■ If including any criticisms of the text, recap some discursive words and phrases that will help children balance positive and negative comments (e.g. *although, however, on the other hand, in contrast*).

■ Remind children that the author should be referred to either as 'the author' or by name.

■ Take each subheading in turn and decide with the children how to sequence the points. Does each require one paragraph or two?

■ Spend some time working on how to express opinions appropriately and clearly, further refining children's ideas and responses to the text in the process. This can be done through discussion (asking 'Do you mean/think ...?' to help children clarify the points). You could continue this in the next session.

Recommendation

■ Remind children that the recommendation sums up their opinions, so it needs to be brief and concise. Given the purpose of the review, it should be upbeat and positive. If they have mentioned some weaknesses, they might want to begin with a phrase like *in spite of ...* .

- Work from your planning notes to draft this section. Decide whether to mention the target readership within the main text or in brackets at the end.

- Tell children that they are now going to draft their own book reviews.

Group follow-up activities   **red/blue/yellow**

Children draft their own texts. They can work alone, in pairs or in groups.

Guided group support

Red Help children to decide how to sequence the information and opinions they want to communicate.

Blue Encourage children to prioritise the information they want to communicate, and to give reasons for their opinions based on evidence from the text.

Yellow As for the blue group. Also, encourage the children to experiment with different ways of expressing opinions and structuring paragraphs.

Plenary Ask for volunteers to share their drafts with the class. Facilitate a 'workshop' discussion in which children praise the strengths of each other's work, and suggest improvements for any weaknesses. Use this discussion to establish some redrafting and editing focuses for the next session. You might choose one or more of the following:

- how to organise the work into clear paragraphs, presenting associated ideas together and separating out any particularly important focuses;

- how to make 'tactful but telling' criticisms within a review which is favourable overall;

- how to 'zap up' the language with powerful adjectives to describe the book in an appealing way and to infer additional praise for the text;

- how to include references to the author.

 Revising and editing the book review

Objectives To improve the text, sharpening its impact on the intended audience

To ensure spelling is accurate and punctuation is effective

Shared session *You need: draft class review, coloured pen (different colour from those used in Session 3).*

*See **Revising and editing** on page 7 for more detailed advice.*

- Tell children that you are going to revise, edit and improve your class review.

- Read through the first draft of their review. Encourage children to try to see the text through the eyes of the intended audience. Does the text meet the reader's needs?

- Keep referring to the original plan to check that all the information has been included and that the intended effect of each section has been fully realised. Experiment with changing some words and some sentence types to see whether improvements can be made.

- Use any focuses agreed during the previous plenary session to guide your revision (e.g. paragraphing, references to the author, use of powerful words and phrases). Shape the session by taking each focus in turn and tracking it through the text from beginning to end.

- Tell children that they are now going to revise their own reviews.

Group follow-up activities

red/blue/yellow

Children work on refining their texts, concentrating on the revision and editing focuses discussed and agreed in the shared session. Alternatively, you may wish to give children individual revision focuses.

Guided group support

Red Help less confident writers by praising the strengths of their work, but tactfully point out some weaknesses too, along with suggested ways of improving them. If necessary, offer one or two alternatives for children to choose from. Take only as much editorial responsibility as needed to ensure that pupils have a finished product they can be proud of.

Blue As for the red group. Challenge children to refine and improve the text. Ask questions that prompt children to reconsider their writing by thinking of the needs of their audience.

Yellow Challenge the most able writers to evaluate their own work, comparing it to published examples. Respond to other children's writing as if you were the target reader to help them examine whether or not they have achieved their intended effect.

Plenary

Ask children to contribute specific examples of improvements they have made in their own texts. Alternatively, if they are struggling to improve a particular part of their text, encourage them to explain the problem and ask for help from the rest of the class.

5 Publishing the book review

Objective

To publish the texts in an appropriate form for the agreed audience

Shared session

You need: revised class review draft, large sheet of paper, coloured pens.

See **Publishing** on page 8 for more detailed notes on the issues involved in the final presentation of the text.

■ Tell children you are now ready to publish your class review, and the review collection containing everybody's work.

■ First, look at how to lay out the class review. Ask children to think of a suitable title. Consider how and where to position the bibliographical data (i.e. publisher, year of publication). Do children think it would help to include some illustrations? What would they include and where would they be positioned?

■ Consider whether to produce a single collection of reviews, or a number of smaller collections grouped by theme/genre. If children choose to produce a single collection, then discuss how they will order the reviews: by theme/genre; alphabetically by title? Will they include a contents page; an index of titles and authors featured?

■ Draw up a rough page plan for the collection.

■ Decide on a title for your collection and discuss a design for the cover. What information needs to be included on the cover? Can children think of ways of making the cover reflect the content, whilst making potential readers want to pick up and read the book? They should bear in mind their target audience.

Some authors and their publishers might be pleased to receive children's reviews of their work. Do check with the publisher before you suggest this option to the class.

■ Discuss how you might circulate the collection (e.g. by placing copies in the school library and with other classes). You might want to consider submitting reviews to a book website for publication online.

Group follow-up activities   **red/blue/yellow**

Children work to produce a final copy of their review.

Guided group support

Red Encourage children to think about how to highlight the title, the bibliographical details (publisher, author's name, etc.) and other key details (e.g. target readership age).

Blue Encourage children to experiment with fonts and type sizes to make the review both eye-catching and clear to read.

Yellow Challenge this group to include an illustration (selected from the book if appropriate) depicting what they think is the key moment in the book, and to write a dramatic caption for it.

Plenary   Share and celebrate the finished texts, enjoying them together. Nothing fuels the next writing project like the success of the last one!

Discuss how to produce the final collection. You could allocate specific tasks to different groups of children (e.g. making the contents and index pages; mounting the reviews on individual pages, binding the book, designing the cover).

If you have submitted the class review to a website, log on to see the published version. You may even have some responses from other readers! Alternatively, discuss how the children feel about exposing their work to worldwide scrutiny. What do they think of other children's work on the website?

ADDITIONAL SESSIONS

Keeping a reading journal

Objectives   To use a reading journal effectively to elicit and record personal responses to a book

To prepare to discuss/write a book review and blurb

Shared session   *You need: copymaster 18 (enlarged to A2/A3), coloured pens.*

The children will probably have a record of the books they have read at home, in class or for guided reading, and may also have kept more detailed reading logs/journals (see **Cornerstones for Writing** *Year 5 Units 1 and 5). These give children the opportunity to reflect on the books they have read, and to respond to the text. You may wish to do this session in advance of Session 2 to ensure the children have a good basis for writing their reviews and blurbs.*

- Display the enlarged copymaster 18 and discuss how to use this before, during and after reading. Model how to use the reading journal framework with a current shared book.

- Complete the first section (reason for choosing book), discussing with the children what are the most important factors for them (e.g. cover (title, illustration, blurb), a familiar author, recommendation in a review or from a teacher or friend).

- Ask about the characters in the shared book and discuss what the children like/dislike about them. Stress the importance of justifying their responses with reference to the text. Write up children's responses on the framework.

- Ask children to suggest ways of building up a character profile in their reading journals (e.g. list of words used by the writer, examples of description/action/ dialogue, an annotated drawing). Point out that this can be added to as they read through the book and get to know more about the character.

- Complete the 'Plot' section with a timeline or flowchart of the events so far, indicating the passage of time between each main event. Elicit some of the most exciting/interesting moments from the children, making sure they give reasons for their responses.

■ Evaluate the strengths and weaknesses of the shared text and write children's responses in the relevant boxes. Ask children what they liked best about the book, and if there was anything they would change. Would they recommend it to other readers? Why/why not?

Group follow-up activities

This is an ongoing task to be completed during independent activity time in the Literacy hour, in silent reading time, as a guided session or at home.

1 red   pupil's book page 54   copymaster 18

Children complete the reading journal framework on the copymaster.

Guided group support

Choose an appropriate focus for each session as the reading journal progresses. Make sure the children develop the habit of always referring to the text to back up their opinions.

2 blue/yellow   pupil's book pages 54–55

Children make their own reading journal by answering a list of questions as they read through their books.

Guided group support As for the red group.

How to write a book blurb

Objectives   To identify key structural and linguistic features of a book blurb

To plan and draft a text for a particular audience and purpose

To select and prioritise information

To write a successful synopsis that gives key information and raises the reader's interest without giving too much away

To write in a dramatic style, choosing vocabulary and phrasing for maximum effect

Shared session (1)   *You need: OHT/poster 25, paper to mask the text, large piece of paper, coloured pens.*

In advance of this session, it would be helpful if children could gather real book blurbs and be prepared to say why they think they are effective/ineffective. (See **Homework suggestions** *on page 103.)*

It would be preferable if you could use the same book that you reviewed in the main unit. Alternatively, use another recently read class text.

■ In this session you will be identifying the key features of a book blurb. Begin with a discussion about what makes a good blurb. You could ask children to read some of the examples they've chosen at this point or just to recall their own experiences of being influenced by blurbs. Recap on the purpose of a blurb (to raise interest, to promote the book, to make you want to read the book).

■ Tell children that they will be writing a back cover blurb themselves. Establish a real purpose and audience for the blurb (e.g. it could be used for a library or classroom display).

■ Now display the first four lines of OHT/poster 25 (mask the rest of the text). What sort of book do children think this is? Who might it appeal to? What does this extract tell the reader about the characters, their situation and the plot?

■ What do children think is the purpose of including part of the text in a blurb? (It gives a flavour of the style of the writing, so readers have an additional indication of whether they are likely to enjoy reading the whole story; it aims to 'hook' the reader's interest.) Ask what is the effect of the extract on OHT/poster 25 (an urgent conversation between two as yet unknown characters, it hints at exciting events and ends with a dramatic exclamation).

■ How many children know this book? Which of those who don't would like to read it, having read just this dialogue? Label this opening section 'Text extract'.

- Display and read the second section. What is its purpose? (To give a brief, tantalising 'taste' of the contents, to raise the reader's interest.) Does it summarise the whole plot? (No, it just gives an outline.) Label this section 'Synopsis'.

- Ask children to tell you all the information given about <u>who</u> the book is about, <u>where</u> the action takes place and <u>what</u> is going on. List their comments on a large sheet of paper headed 'Key information'. Organise the notes under headings ('Situation/problem', 'Plot – key events', 'Characters', 'Setting').

- Ask children to identify key language features (present tense, informal language, for example *on the run*). Look at how concisely information about the story is given. For example, *Penniless and parentless* sums up the <u>result</u> of key events not described. (Note the use of alliteration here.)

- Ask the children to identify and underline all the 'punchy' and dramatic words used and to discuss their impact. Thinking of alternatives may help to highlight the impact made (e.g. why did the writer choose *tyrannical* rather than just *cruel*; *faith*, rather than *belief*?).

- How does the blurb end? (With a final 'hook' to make the reader want to know what happens next.) Discuss whether the writer could have added an ellipsis here (*if they are ever to reach their destination ...*). Ask why these are so often found in blurbs (they provide another way of inviting readers to speculate about what might happen next).

- Display the quotes at the bottom of OHT/poster 25. Ask the children what these are (review quotes) and label them as such. Who do children think they are aimed at: adults or children (or both)? (Mainly at adults buying books for children, for example librarians (one quote is from *School Librarian*), teachers, parents.) Ask whether the children are ever influenced by the review quotes on back covers.

- Ask who will have selected these quotes (the publisher). What is their purpose? (To promote the book, to persuade the reader to buy it.) Explain that publishers try to choose the most persuasive quotes from the most impressive sources. Ensure that children can see that the first quote praises the story itself (*a wonderful tale*), whilst the second praises the literary quality (*writing at its best*).

- Can the children spot that one of the quotes provides an additional detail about the book? (We learn from the first quote that Kush is *a performing elephant*.)

Group follow-up activities (1)

1 red   pupil's book page 56

Children now analyse a blurb from *South By South East* by Anthony Horowitz and list the key information.

Guided group support Help children to identify and assess the impact of 'hook' (dramatic and strong) words in the text. Encourage them to decide whether or not they would read this book, and why. Help them to identify three key elements in the blurb (text extract, synopsis, recommendation).

2 blue   pupil's book pages 56–57

Children analyse blurbs from *South By South East* by Anthony Horowitz and *The Illustrated Mum* by Jacqueline Wilson and list the key information from each. They also consider some questions about the blurb.

Guided group support As for the red group. Help children to consider the additional questions if they find these difficult.

3 yellow   pupil's book page 57

Children analyse blurbs from *The Illustrated Mum* by Jacqueline Wilson and *Harry Potter and the Prisoner of Azkaban* by J.K. Rowling.

Guided group support Encourage children to compare the three blurbs and to decide which book they would prefer to read, giving reasons for their preference.

Plenary (1) Create a class poster entitled 'How to write a successful book blurb'. Ask children to tell you what they have learnt about successful blurb writing and make notes (e.g. use strong, 'punchy' words; include a dramatic text extract; end with a hint of exciting events to come). Ensure that the four main sections of a blurb are included (text extract, synopsis, recommendation, review quotes). Ask for feedback on each blurb studied, encouraging children to compare and contrast the different blurbs and evaluate their impact and effectiveness in raising the reader's interest. Add to the class poster any further points that arise from the discussion.

Shared session (2) *You need: 'How to write a successful book blurb' poster, large sheets of paper, coloured pens.*

Before this session, set groups of children the task of finding a suitable opening text extract from the book you will be writing a blurb for. Remind them that this should be very short, dramatic and intriguing. If necessary, dialogue could be extracted from a longer passage.

The planning and drafting steps may be taken together or split over two sessions.

■ In this session you will be planning and writing the blurb. Ensure that pupils understand that a back cover blurb for a children's story may be short, but is actually a very sophisticated piece of writing, which has to be carefully planned and executed.

■ Briefly recap what children have learnt about blurbs, referring to the class poster.

■ Create a simple framework that will help children to plan their own writing. Draw four large, rectangular boxes on a sheet of paper and ask what these might contain, writing in children's comments:

  ○ A text extract (giving a flavour of the voice and style of the text; should be dramatic, intriguing).

  ○ A very brief synopsis (giving details of <u>who</u>, <u>where</u> and <u>what</u>; should be aimed at children who may read the book).

  ○ A recommendation (a persuasive statement; should suggest target readership).

  ○ Review quotes (to emphasise the good qualities of the book; mainly aimed at adults buying for children).

■ Remind pupils again of the purpose of writing a blurb, and of the audience – or audiences – for whom this particular blurb is intended.

■ Ask children to suggest some text extracts which could be used in your blurb (see marginal note above) and to give reasons for their choices. The class can then vote for the best one. Keep relating any decisions made to the impact we want the text to have on the audience.

■ Next, brainstorm essential information about characters, setting and main events to include in the synopsis. Make notes on a separate large sheet of paper. Identify the most important information, decide on topics for each paragraph and the order in which they should appear.

■ Ask for three positive adjectives that sum up the book, for use in the recommendation section.

■ Decide how many review quotes should be included for adult appeal. Identify a small number of key points which these should focus on.

■ Check back over the plan to ensure that the text is adequately represented.

■ You are now ready to begin drafting the synopsis. Work through the paragraphs one at a time, challenging children to find ways of linking information into pacy, concise, high-impact sentences. If required, use a thesaurus to find the most powerful synonyms for what you are trying to convey. Try varying the sentence type for effect, using questions, statements and two- or three-word exclamations. Keep reading aloud as you work, to ensure that children can see, hear, and really feel the effect of the writing.

■ Consider the ending of the synopsis: you could end with an intriguing question or an ellipsis to raise suspense.

- When drafting a persuasive statement for the recommendation section, select powerful vocabulary as above and settle for one or two statements which are likely to be widely appealing to the target age group (children). You may wish to consider the appropriateness of using colloquial expressions, or high-impact words 'borrowed' from the text to express your opinions.

- Encourage the class to have fun composing more formal persuasive statements designed to appeal to parents and teachers. Do they think a recommendation from a head teacher would carry weight? (If so, your own Head might oblige!)

- Make up some appropriate review quotes (you could include a quote from the class review if your blurb is for the same book).

Group follow-up activities (2)   **4 red/blue/yellow   pupil's book page 58**

Children plan and draft their own blurbs for a book of their choice. They can work alone, in pairs or in groups, as directed by you.

Guided group support

Red Help children to prioritise information and shape it effectively into a blurb, using the framework from the shared session. (You can cut down this framework, for example to contain just the synopsis and persuasive statement.)

Blue Encourage children to think of their audience when choosing the information to include in their synopsis. Challenge them to choose dramatic, 'high impact' words and phrases.

Yellow Encourage children to experiment with different sentence types, making use of questions, varying sentence length and including short exclamations. Help them to choose different registers of vocabulary for the review quotes.

Plenary (2)   Conduct a 'thinking aloud' session in which children contribute examples of particular problems or successes encountered during planning or drafting. Note on the 'How to write a successful book blurb' poster any important and helpful points that arise. You could also invite volunteers to read aloud what they have written so far. Encourage positive feedback from the class.

Consider producing final copies of your blurb on paper folded to resemble a book jacket, perhaps featuring the book title attractively illustrated on the 'front cover'. Alternatively, children's work could be produced on A4 sheets and bound into a simple book to go on the shelf alongside the text or texts for which the blurbs were written.

 Annotating a passage of text in response to a specific question

Objectives   To be able to identify specific elements of text that create particular effects on the reader

To be able to justify an opinion, analysis or evaluation with reference to textual evidence

Shared session   *You need: OHT/poster 26, 3 different coloured pens.*

- As part of keeping a reading journal, it may be valuable to teach pupils how to select and annotate a passage to develop a specific line of enquiry. In this session, the children will investigate the following question:

    'How does J.K. Rowling create and sustain the magical world that Harry Potter finds at Hogwarts School?'

Write this question up so that the children can see it.

- Display and read OHT/poster 26. Ask the children whether they think it does, indeed, paint a magical picture.

- Explain that this is the first time Harry enters the Great Hall, and that the first sentence of the passage reminds us of this in a very direct way. Ask children to listen as you re-read the paragraph, and try to picture in their own imaginations how it must have looked to Harry. Ask them to try and identify the 'trigger' words that the author has placed in the text as a means of eliciting or provoking a particular reaction in the mind of a reader.

- Point out that the author represents the hall as seen through Harry's eyes. Ask the children to identify and underline all the references to eyes, staring, seeing or looking. Furthermore, the picture of the Hall that the author creates is almost literally 'lit up' in the mind of the reader by repeated references to sources of light. Ask children to identify and underline these (*thousands and thousands of candles, glittering golden plates, faces … like pale lanterns in the flickering candlelight, ghosts shone misty silver, stars*).

- Harry's initial reaction is that the hall is both *strange* and *splendid*. Help children to realise that the author uses these adjectives to set the tone of the description even before giving any details. Ask the children to track down the subsequent supporting evidence for each of these words, using different coloured pens to mark them (strange things: candles floating in mid-air, ghosts among the students, stars on the ceiling, a bewitched ceiling; splendid things: all those candles, glittering gold tableware, ghosts shining with a silvery light, a black velvet ceiling, stars on the ceiling). Below is an example of how the text could be annotated (the 'eye' icon denotes references to seeing and looking mentioned earlier):

---

we are told how to feel about the hall. Strong words   light

Harry had never even imagined such a strange and splendid place. It was lit
effective repetition   light   very strange!
by **thousands and thousands** of candles which were floating in mid-air over

four long tables, where the rest of the students were sitting. These tables were
light   very rich and regal
laid with glittering golden plates and goblets. At the top of the Hall was

another long table where the teachers were sitting. Professor McGonagall led

the first-years up here, so that they came to a halt in a line facing the other
big number—overwhelming
students, with the teachers behind them. The hundreds of faces staring at
light
them looked like pale lanterns in the flickering candlelight. Dotted here and
mystery   light   more precious metal
there among the students, the ghosts shone misty silver. Mainly to avoid all
luxury material
the staring eyes, Harry looked upwards, and saw a velvety black ceiling dotted
light   mystery
with stars. He heard Hermione whisper, "It's bewitched to look like the sky

outside, I read about it in *Hogwarts, a History*."

- Were the children surprised to discover how much is going on in such a short piece of text? Tell them that they are now going to look at some more passages from Harry Potter books.

Group follow-up activities

Extracts for the following activities appear both in the pupil's book and on the copymasters.

1 red   pupil's book page 59   copymaster 19

Pupils read and annotate the extract. They identify the words and ideas that make a game of Quidditch seem so different and magical.

Guided group support Encourage children to articulate <u>why</u> the words and phrases they have underlined have the effect that they do.

2 blue   pupil's book page 60   copymaster 20

Pupils read and annotate the extract. They analyse how the author combines special or magical elements with everyday elements.

Guided group support As for the red group.

3 yellow   pupil's book page 61   copymaster 21

Pupils read and annotate the extract. They identify elements which build up suspense as a new character is introduced and contrast this with the anti-climax as the character speaks.

Guided group support As for the red group.

Plenary

Encourage children to share the insights they have gained from annotating their texts. Help them to see how analysing a text like this helps them to become more involved with the text. What have they learnt about J.K. Rowling's skills as a writer?

Writing a series of linked haiku

Objectives

To explore a particular form of poetry and its conventions

To write in a particular form

To create a series of linked poems

Shared session

You need: OHT/poster 27, large sheet of paper, coloured pens.

The following material could be spread over two sessions if necessary.

■ Read and enjoy the model haiku on OHT/poster 27 with children. Point out that the poems all have in common the concept of rain, but offer very different viewpoints.

■ Discuss what children already know of the form. Revise the major points about haiku:

 ○ they originate from Japan;
 ○ they are becoming increasingly popular in English poetry;
 ○ they have three lines;
 ○ the first and third lines have five syllables, the second has seven;
 ○ they offer a 'glimpse' of the subject, rather than trying to describe it completely;
 ○ they are valued for their lightness of touch.

■ Discuss in detail the images they paint, and the feelings they convey. Investigate how much they state and how much they merely hint at. For example, what would a full moon look like if surrounded by a *halo/shining cool benevolence*? What does this have to do with the promise of rain? Look at the image of *Gently pattering/rain, dropping from rose petals*: do children find this easier to understand? But what does the word 'soft' add to the meaning? How does the image of *a mother's tears* change the feelings of the reader towards the rain?

- Talk with pupils about the advantages and disadvantages of the haiku form. Focusing on its length and its ability to communicate, compare and contrast with other forms (e.g. ballad, elegy). Use whatever recent experience the class has had with poetry of all kinds.

- Find out whether pupils like the haiku form or not, and why.

- Explain that a series of haiku can be linked together to form what is called a **renga**. A renga is a series of haiku linked by two lines of seven syllables each. Traditionally, a renga would be written by more than one poet – each adding another haiku to the chain, which could continue until there were up to 100 haiku in total!

- Suggest to the class that it would be fun to write a series of haiku, linked with two additional lines into a continuous renga. This could be a based upon a familiar coherent unit with several parts (e.g. days of the week, months of the year, seasons, aspects of weather). Suggest also that, to blend Eastern and Western styles together, you could compose a repetitive refrain of two seven-syllable lines as the link between each haiku.

- Identify how, where and when the poems will be published or displayed. Establish the subject. This should be one about which all pupils can contribute a point of view or an image. (The notes which follow will focus on seasons of the year, but you may choose another topic.)

- Try to write at least two verses and a refrain in the shared session, to give pupils a chance to practise their haiku/renga writing skills in preparation for the independent writing task which follows.

- Talk with the class about the characteristics of Spring – mild weather, buds, flowers, lambs, rain showers. Focus children on an image of Spring (e.g. blue skies; a bright yellow sun and white clouds reflected in little puddles; a tree without leaves, but covered in blossom; green grass). It may prove most fruitful to encourage the children to present 5-syllable 'snapshots' of what can be seen in the mind's eye when Spring is considered in this way, for example:

  > pink blossoms, blue skies
  > delicate petals
  > sunbeams chase raindrops
  > sunshine on water
  > rainbows in blue skies
  > buds of tender green
  > grass reaching upwards
  > green buds bring forth joy

- Emphasise that the haiku form is almost grammar-free, and can just offer a series of glimpses and feelings, informally organised and punctuated.

- The 7-syllable lines could be used to communicate a 'feeling' of the season, sandwiched between two visual images. Some examples:

  > new life wakes beneath the soil
  > winter's long sleep now ending
  > warmth brings time to grow again
  > the joy of recreation

- Here is an example verse about Spring, created in this way:

  > Sunbeams chase raindrops,
  > new life wakes beneath the soil,
  > green buds bring forth joy.

■ The next haiku – about Summer – could be created in the same way:

> Gold sun, sapphire skies,
> the glories of nature are
> bright, multi-coloured.

Revision and editing: in haiku, there is relatively little material, so this is unlikely to be too time-consuming. Help children to read through the drafts to ensure that the 'flavour' of each verse is different enough to reflect its subject as the poem moves through the seasons. Ensure that visual images are clearly portrayed in the two five-syllable lines and that the 'feeling' or 'atmosphere' of each season is elicited in the seven-syllable line.

■ Look at how the verses could be linked. Remember that this requires two lines of seven syllables. In this example, an observation on the changing nature of the seasons would be appropriate, perhaps including a reference to the cycle of life:

> Round and round the planet spins,
> life ebbs and flows, ongoing.

Or

> Within the seasons' cycle,
> life and death are eternal.

■ Experiment with different combinations of ideas and images until you have a usable link that contributes something meaningful, or adds a larger dimension to the overall theme of the work.

■ Tell children they are now going to write their own haiku.

Group follow-up session

red/blue/yellow

Children work on their own haiku. It could either be linked to the one that has just been done in the shared session (e.g. they might work on autumn or winter), or you could allocate different subjects within a series to different children. Having completed their own haiku, pupils can swap work with a writing partner and compose responses, as in the traditional Japanese style.

Guided group support

Red Help children to see an image in their mind's eye, which they can attempt to describe in detail (colours, shapes, sizes, feelings). Establish the communicative power of so few syllables.

Blue/yellow Encourage children to focus on a freeze-frame image when they write their own haiku.

Plenary Ask for volunteers from each group to read out their poems, with their partner reading the response (if one was written).

Homework suggestions

- Keep a reading journal of your current reading book. **(After Session 1)**

- Imagine that a neighbour has to spend some time in hospital and has asked you to go to the library and select two or three books for them to read. Compile a list of questions you will need to ask to find out about their taste in reading. Think about types of story, favourite authors, etc. **(After Session 1)**

- Interview two friends or relatives about the best and the worst books they have ever read. Make notes of the questions you ask to find out why they feel this way. Make notes also of what they say in reply. Write a brief report about each for inclusion in a class anthology of 'Best Books'. **(After Session 2)**

- Write a plot synopsis of a book you have read recently. **(After Session 2)**

- Ask six children what they think makes a book 'good'. Ask them to name two good books. Ask six adults how they would judge whether a book would be 'good' for children. Ask them to name two good books each. Write a report setting out both responses and listing the texts chosen. If you have time, read and review one book from each side of the list. **(After Session 3)**

- Gather some blurbs from real books and take them into school for a class discussion. Think about whether the blurbs are effective or not. **(Before 'How to write a book blurb')**

- Pick six books at random from the library shelves. Read the blurbs and think about whether they make you want to read the books. Put the books in order, from the one that seems the most interesting to the one that seems the least interesting. Photocopy or copy out the first and the last blurbs. Write about why they did or did not work for you. **(After 'How to write a book blurb')**

- Think of a good book you have read recently. Think of ten persuasive things you could say about it to make a friend read it too. Choose a short passage from the book that gives a 'flavour' of what makes it so good. Copy it out and add your own illustration if you want to. Give it to your friend … and see if it works! **(After 'How to write a book blurb')**

UNIT **5**   How to write a book review

Colour the right number of stars to show how well you did the following things:

0 stars = I didn't do it.   3 stars = I did it well.
1 star = I gave it a try.   4 stars = I did an excellent job!
2 stars = I did it quite well.

I kept a reading journal over an extended period of time.	☆	☆	☆	☆
I responded in depth and detail to one or more texts.	☆	☆	☆	☆
I gave my opinion and justified it with reference to the text.	☆	☆	☆	☆
My review gives readers clear information about the book.	☆	☆	☆	☆
My review inspired others to read the book.	☆	☆	☆	☆
I learnt how to write a clear, brief synopsis.	☆	☆	☆	☆
My blurb persuaded others to read the book.	☆	☆	☆	☆

Something I am especially pleased with

Something my audience liked in my writing

Something I'd like to do better next time

Term three non-fiction focus:
6 How to write explanations for different audiences and purposes

What most children will already know:

That causal and chronological connectives create cohesion and sequence within explanation texts

That order and sequence are achieved in non-chronological report texts through the use of clear and helpful headings

That many information texts contain a mix of both of these main text types

That paragraphs are used to organise and present information clearly

What they will learn in this unit:

How to supplement report text with elements of explanation

How to incorporate explanations into different information texts

How to write and present information texts for specific purposes and audiences

 Structure and language

Objectives
To identify the key features of non-chronological report texts

To identify the key features of explanation texts

To investigate how these are combined in an information text for a particular purpose and audience

Shared session
You need: OHTs/posters 28 and 29, 3 different coloured pens, large sheet of paper.

■ Display OHTs/posters 28 and 29. Can children deduce just from the appearance and layout where this text might be from, who it is written for and what is its purpose? (It is a page from a science textbook for Years 7–8.) Read the text together and ask them to identify the two main text types used (report and explanation).

■ Ask children to identify one paragraph which is a good example of explanatory text (the 'Photosynthesis' section). Draw a box around it and label it 'explanation'.

■ What distinguishing features helped them to identify it? (Use of chronological connectives (e.g. *At the same time, then*) and causal connectives (e.g. *because, So*).) Underline these. Did the children identify the annotated diagram as being part of the explanation?

■ Now ask the children to look at the rest of the text to find examples of typical features of a non-chronological report (layout, with headings, sub-headings, bullet points; use of the present tense; impersonal language; generalised plural nouns (e.g. *plants, roots*) and technical vocabulary (e.g. *constituents*)). Underline or label these.

■ What is the purpose of the title and first short paragraph? (To introduce the subject briefly, preparing the reader for what they are to learn.) Recap that this is typical of both report and explanatory texts.

■ Then look at the facts reported in the following three paragraphs. Why is it helpful that these are presented in three separate paragraphs? (This helps to organise the information, and the sub-headings make the subject of each paragraph clear at a glance.) Could this section have been laid out differently (e.g. using bullet points)?

*You could build a glossary for this text as a homework activity. (See **Homework suggestions** on page 114.)*

■ Ask why some words are highlighted in bold (these are key words that the reader may not know, included in the glossary). Are there any other words that the children would like to have glossed?

■ Did the children already know about photosynthesis? Do they think the author assumes the reader does? What does the author do before explaining it? (Establishes some basic facts required to understand it.) Make sure children see that the author has considered the reader's needs.

■ Finally, look at the last two paragraphs. What is their purpose? (To explain what happens if any of the three conditions are lacking.) Why has the author used bullet points to list the effects? (To make the information concise and easier to memorise.) Recap that this is a useful device when writing both reports and explanations.

■ Did the children find this text clear and easy to follow? To establish how effective it is as a teaching text, ask them to tell you what they have learnt about plants from reading it and invite volunteers to explain photosynthesis. Then ask which features particularly aided their understanding (e.g. the diagram, highlighted key words, bullet-pointed text). Remind children that an explanation is often included within a report to help the reader to understand a difficult or important concept.

Group follow-up activities

1 red/blue/yellow   pupil's book page 62

Children find examples of the key features of a non-chronological report and identify the explanatory section, noting some of its key features.

Guided group support Revise points from the shared session as necessary, making sure that the children can relate them to the new text. Ensure that they are clear about how report and explanation text work together to aid the reader's understanding (e.g. the fact that viruses are a type of microbe is established *before* the explanation about cold viruses).

2 blue/yellow   pupil's book page 63

Children read an explanatory text, then write a short explanation about why it is important to wash your hands before touching food.

Guided group support Encourage children to adapt the structure of the text to suit the audience's needs. How might they alter their text to suit the needs of younger children?

3 yellow   pupil's book page 63

If time, children build a glossary of technical vocabulary and other key words found in the texts. They can work as a group or in pairs.

Guided group support Challenge children to word their explanations as clearly as possible to help a younger reader to understand.

Plenary   Create a class poster entitled 'How to write an explanation text'. Divide the poster into two columns and entitle the first 'Non-chronological report with explanation'. Ask children to recap on the features of both non-chronological reports and explanation texts. Then ask them to describe how <u>explanation</u> can be used within a non-chronological report to support learning (e.g. to explain a difficult or new concept) and how <u>report</u> text can support an explanation (e.g. to present important facts clearly and concisely to aid understanding). Write up their responses on the poster.

(2) Using explanations for different audiences and purposes

Objectives   To recognise that the same information can be presented differently for different purposes and audiences

To show how explanations can be usefully incorporated into different kinds of text

Shared session   *You need: OHTs/posters 28, 29 and 30, 'How to write an information text' poster (from Session 1), large piece of paper, coloured pens.*

■   Display OHTs/posters 28 and 29. Tell the children that they are going to buy a houseplant at a local garden centre. They need to know how to look after the plant. Would they find this text helpful? How would they change it (e.g. adapt the text to form a series of instructions)? Write up their ideas.

■   Now display and read OHT/poster 30, which the garden centre has included with the plant. Is this text more helpful? Help children to understand that much of the same information is included here, but within a different text type (instruction).

■   Focus on the use of *you* in the opening passage. Why do they think this text starts in this informal way? (This friendly, personal touch is likely to appeal to anxious beginner gardeners who might be daunted by a very formal, impersonal introduction.) Encourage the children to notice that once the audience link has been established, the style becomes more formal.

■   Ask children to highlight where and why explanations are given (e.g. in the first instruction and the 'Warning' section; to reinforce the importance of following the instructions; to explain extra details). Do children think that people are more likely to carry out instructions if they know <u>why</u> they are important?

■   Invite children to look for more places in the text where it would be helpful to include some explanation. Based on what they have learnt from the previous text on green plants, what might the explanations say? (We could add 'Light gives energy for photosynthesis' to the second instruction; or 'As plants grow towards the light, you need to turn them so that they keep a balanced shape' to the third.)

■   Ask whether the text is laid out and presented clearly. Remind children of the audience and purpose. Is there anything lacking (e.g. would more pictures be helpful)? Could symbols replace some of the text? Would bullet points or sub-headings be helpful? Spend some time discussing different ideas.

Group follow-up activities   **1 red   pupil's book page 64**

Children read some fire safety instructions, and highlight explanatory text. They then add their own explanations to a second set of instructions.

Guided group support Once the children have decided where explanations are appropriate and what they should say, help them to link them to the text with appropriate causal connectives (e.g. *this is because ...*; *so that ...*).

2 blue   pupil's book page 65

Children add explanations to a series of instructions for dealing with a blocked escape route.

Guided group support As for the red group. If time, ask children to think of instructions for preventing a house fire, including explanations.

3 yellow   pupil's book page 65

Children write a set of instructions for dealing with a fire in school, adding explanations wherever appropriate.

Guided group support Encourage children to organise their instructions under appropriate sub-headings.

Plenary Return to the 'How to write an information text' poster, and entitle the second column 'Instruction text with explanations'. Ask the children to describe how explanations can support instructions (e.g. to explain <u>why</u> something is important, to increase the reader's understanding and awareness) and note their answers. Invite volunteers to read out their fire safety instructions and then discuss them. Are they clear to follow? Are there any exceptions to the rule that need explaining? If you have a copy of the school's fire safety instructions, compare these with the children's. Discuss where the explanations are genuinely helpful and where they may be simply stating the obvious!

③ Using the passive in explanation texts

Objectives To investigate the effect of including or excluding personal language in information texts

To reinforce understanding of the use of the passive voice

Shared session *You need: OHTs/posters 31 and 32.*

Children should have been introduced to the passive voice through sentence-level work in Year 6, Terms 1 and 2. However, you may wish to do some extra practice or revision before this session. You might find it helpful to refer to the flow chart provided on page 67 of the pupil's book.

- Tell children that in this session you are going to explore some characteristics of formal writing for different purposes and audiences.

- First, write up the following, inviting children to discuss in pairs whether there are any differences between the pairs of sentences.

> You must water this plant regularly.
> This plant must be watered regularly.

> A plant takes in water through its roots.
> Water is taken in through a plant's roots.

Elicit from the children that, in each case, the pairs of sentences mean more or less the same. However, what differences did they spot? (They may be able to point out that the first sentence of each pair is 'active' while the second is 'passive'.)

- Focus on the first pair. Elicit from children that the first sentence is an instruction, using direct, personal language (*You*); the second is more indirect, presenting the same information as a fact (in the style of a report text). Which is more formal in style? Recap that a formal text avoids using personal words like *you*. Ensure that pupils are aware that use of the passive in formal texts – particularly scientific texts – transfers attention away from the <u>doer</u> (the agent) and onto <u>what has been done</u>. It is an accepted convention of scientific text that it is the <u>science</u>, not the scientist, that is of most importance. In the first sentence, the use of *you* makes it clear whose responsibility the watering must be. The more formal second sentence, in the passive voice, simply indicates that it must be done, without suggesting who should do it. Pupils may have opinions about which of these is likely to prove more effective in securing water for the plant!

- Now display the first two extracts on OHT/poster 31 and ask which is more formal. Recap that the second extract is deliberately more informal and 'friendly', as it is meant to appeal directly to the houseplant buyer.

- Focus on the second pair of sentences given above. Elicit from the children that there is a difference in emphasis: ask which is the most important element in each, the plant or water (in the first, the plant; in the second, water). Which do the children think would be more appropriate for a very formal text? (Passive sentences <u>tend</u> to be used in more formal texts.)

- Now display the final two extracts on OHT/poster 31. Go through each with the children, asking them to pick out and underline examples of the passive. Which do they think is the more formal text and why?

- Next, display and read OHT/poster 32. Explain that this is an entry from a scientist's diary. If they were the scientist, what changes would children have to make to turn this into a formal piece of scientific writing? (Reinforce their understanding of the use of passive/active language in formal/informal texts.) Start to draft the formal text with the children. Create a main heading and decide whether any sub-headings would be helpful. When you have a rough framework, write the first few sentences together.

Group follow-up activities

1 red   pupil's book page 66

Pupils rewrite an informal, observational recount of a scientific experiment in a formal, impersonal style.

Guided group support Help pupils to sharpen their understanding of formal and informal language features. Focus on the way the single verb in the active form (put) becomes a verb chain (was put) in the passive form.

2 blue/yellow   pupil's book page 67

Pupils read an extract from a formal explanation, changing active sentences into passive ones as appropriate.

Guided group support Find and list the active and passive verbs. Help pupils to identify the precise differences between the constructions. Ensure pupils understand that the use of the passive is a formal literary convention, especially in scientific or technical writing.

Plenary   Allow pupils to conduct a 'quiz challenge' session, taking sentences from their own work for peers to transform from active to passive and vice versa. Try to formulate a class rule about when the passive form can be used. Begin a collection of passive sentences found in reading, and annotate with notes about the text type and the purpose or effect of the text.

Planning a report

Objectives   To draw up an appropriate framework for writing

To write for a particular purpose and audience

Shared session   *You need: large sheet of paper, coloured pens.*

■ Explain that you are now going to write a class information text, related to work children are already doing in another curriculum area (e.g. rivers and the water cycle, if they have covered this in geography).

■ Establish a real purpose and audience (e.g. to write a book for another class or to create a display for a particular area of the school).

■ Brainstorm the content to be covered. Discuss what the audience needs to know and what they might already know. Consider how to make the text interesting and attention-grabbing.

■ List some of the subject-specific vocabulary. Will you need a glossary?

■ At this point, you could discuss research requirements, the use of reference materials and IT. Recap on the need to acknowledge sources in the text.

*If you decide to include a glossary then you may want to shared-write this with the class in a later session. You could set children the task of researching entries for the glossary as a homework or extension activity. (See **Homework suggestions** on page 114.)*

■ Establish the main sections of the writing, which will cover different aspects of the subject, and decide upon a rough order for the information. (Children will be given different sections of this text to write in the guided group activity session. You might want to agree which group will be writing which section at this point.)

■ Now draw up a framework for the first section, which you will write together. Choose which information from the brainstorming session should be included. Ask what can be simply reported and what needs explaining to the reader. Where might pictures and annotated diagrams support the reader?

■ Work on sequencing and organising the information. Ask for suggestions for headings and sub-headings, which you will use to create the planning framework.

■ Tell children they are now going to plan their own section of the text.

Group follow-up activities   **red/blue/yellow**

Working either individually, in pairs or in groups, children create their own framework or writing plan for a given section of the writing (as agreed in the shared session).

Guided group support

Red Help children to keep in mind the needs of their audience when drawing up their framework. In particular, help them to identify where explanation will be useful.

Blue Emphasise the importance of shaping and sequencing the text in a clear and logical way. Help children to identify where explanation will be useful, bearing in mind the needs of the audience.

Yellow As for the blue and red groups. Also, challenge children to extend their plans, ensuring that sufficient detail is presented and that the subject matter is adequately covered. You could also focus on the use of explanatory text in annotated diagrams.

Plenary   Ask for volunteers to share their plans with the class. Compare and contrast two or three plans, asking children to focus on the different ways they meet the needs of the audience. Ask for feedback on which areas were easy to plan, and any elements that caused more difficulty.

5 Drafting the report

Objectives
To use a framework to write for a particular audience and purpose

To use elements of report and explanation in order to present information clearly

To write in an impersonal style, including the passive voice

To write in sequenced and linked paragraphs, using appropriate connectives

Shared session
You need: class framework (from Session 4), 'How to write an information text' poster (from Session 1), coloured pen.

*See **Drafting** on page 7 for more detailed advice on conducting a whole-class drafting session.*

■ Quickly recap on the framework you made during the previous session. Remind the children of the purpose and audience and that the main challenge is now to write the text using appropriate language.

■ Are the children happy with the main heading? Ask them how the text will begin (with a general, introductory paragraph).

■ Recap on which sections are to be reported and which explained and the key difference between the two: the report is non-chronological, defining or classifying something; the explanation gives the 'how' or 'why' about something (often in a sequence of logical steps, linked with chronological or causal connectives).

■ Draft the opening together, revising the conventions of impersonal language, especially how and when to use the passive voice. If you agreed on a class rule for using the passive in Session 3, refer back to this now.

■ As the focus of the text shifts between explanation and report from paragraph to paragraph, revise the main language features of both of the relevant text types (e.g. use of present tense and generalised plural nouns in the report; a greater use of the passive in the explanation).

■ As you write, continue to focus pupils on the conventions of formal writing. If children offer any personal, informal language, help them to see why these might be inappropriate and ask the class to think of more formal alternatives. Encourage frequent use of technical and subject-specific vocabulary. Be prepared to suggest examples of passive sentences to be included.

■ Encourage children to keep bearing in mind the needs of their audience. Ask if any words might need glossing, and how these should be treated – perhaps give an explanation in a box on the page? Think about how the text can be organised and presented to make it clearer (e.g. by using a bulleted list to set out key facts in brief).

■ Tell children they are now going to draft their own section of the text.

Group follow-up activities

red/blue/yellow

Children draft their own texts from their plans.

Guided group support

Red Help children to consolidate their understanding of the differences between reporting and explaining. Encourage oral 'try-outs' in order to establish the voice of the text.

Blue As for the red group. Also, focus pupils on the purpose of each paragraph and help them to sequence and link them logically.

Yellow As for the blue and red groups. Also, challenge children to maintain a formal, impersonal style.

Plenary Ask for volunteers to read out successful sections of their texts for the class to evaluate. Give children an opportunity to discuss any writing problems they may have encountered. Invite children to add anything else they have come to understand about the writing of texts like this to the 'How to write an information text' poster.

6 Revising and editing the report

Objectives To ensure the use of present tense and passive voice is maintained

To ensure that paragraphing has been used to best effect in organising, dividing and presenting ideas

To promote cohesion between paragraphs

Shared session *You need: draft class report, coloured pens (different colour from that used in Session 5).*

*See **Revising and editing** on page 7 for more detailed advice.*

■ Explain that you are going to try to improve the class text, bearing in mind the audience and purpose.

■ Look at the role of each paragraph in the overall shape of the text. Check the content of each paragraph. Ensure that text breaks are appropriately managed, with a shift of idea or emphasis from paragraph to paragraph. Check headings for each section of text and ensure that these are helpful and cohesive. Examine whether headings adequately map out the text at a glance in order to help the reader navigate through the information offered. Carry out 'repairs' as necessary, modelling how to annotate the text with revisions to be made.

■ In report sections, ensure that the facts are presented in a clear and concise way and that headings, sub-headings and bullet points are used where appropriate.

■ In explanation sections, ensure that steps or stages are in a logical order, using appropriate causal or temporal connectives to link them clearly, and that adequate detail is given. Check that the information is organised appropriately into paragraphs.

■ Check that the simple present tense has been used where appropriate, and that any departures from this are properly managed. Ensure that repetitive use of pronouns does not detract from clarity.

■ Briefly discuss the use of bold, italics, caps, etc. to highlight words and headings. For example, if you are including a glossary, how will you highlight the words to be glossed?

■ If any reference sources have been used, how have they been acknowledged in the text? Within the text or in a footnote?

■ Write a list of some specific aspects for the children to focus on when revising their own texts (e.g. headings and sub-headings, paragraphing, use of present tense, use of connectives). If you wish, invite them to choose two of these to concentrate on and to write these at the top of their texts before they start.

Group follow-up activities

red/blue/yellow

Children work independently and/or collaboratively to revise and edit their texts.

Guided group support

Red Encourage children to work in pairs or small groups, and to act as an audience for each other's texts. Ensure that children have sequenced their text logically into paragraphs that are linked with appropriate connectives.

Blue As for the red group. Encourage children to identify two or three parts of the text that could be rewritten to raise the formal, impersonal tone (e.g. by using passive instead of active verbs).

Yellow As for the red and blue groups. Encourage children to think about using stylistic devices (e.g. bold and italics to highlight words) and organisational devices (e.g. sub-headings and bullet points) and to consider how to style any source acknowledgements.

Plenary Invite volunteers to share their texts. Ask them to explain their redrafting focus and to tell the class how they dealt with the weaknesses they found. Encourage others to comment constructively on strengths and weaknesses in their work.

7 Publishing the report

Objective To present text appropriately for audience and purpose

Shared session *You need: revised class report draft, large sheet of paper, coloured pens.*

*See **Publishing** on page 8 for more detailed notes on the issues involved in the final presentation of the text.*

- Briefly discuss how to produce and publish/display the work (e.g. use of word-processing, the style, format and size of the work). Possibilities to consider could include: an information booklet, a large-scale poster, a leaflet or a straightforward A4 word-processed sheet. Decide on the most appropriate form for the text to ensure that it reaches its target audience.

- The more formal the text, the more necessary it is to use ICT to ensure that children's finished work looks the part. The text could be word processed, diagrams could be scanned in, and pupils could experiment with highlighting effects on titles and headings.

- Discuss whether pictures or diagrams might be helpful, and where these should be positioned. Sketch a rough layout on a large sheet of paper.

- How will the work finish? Do you need a final picture or a particularly interesting fact to finish off with?

- Discuss in more detail how you could work on the presentation of the text, drawing upon children's knowledge of text design. How could capitals, bold, italics or spacing be used to make the text clearer?

- How many levels of heading does the text have? Discuss how important, and therefore how prominent, each needs to be and establish a consistent type size and style accordingly. Will you use any colour-coding to guide the reader? Would it be helpful to box off any section of the text? If a glossary is included, how should this be treated? How will the key words be highlighted in the text?

- Tell children they are now going to work on final versions of their sections of the text.

Group follow-up activities

If children will be using a word-processing package, encourage them to experiment with changing the appearance of their own text: changing the highlighting effects on the title, changing the font and type size, trying out different ways of highlighting key words. They should print out the version they think is best, and be ready to explain their design decisions.

red/blue/yellow

Children work on the presentation of their texts to produce a final version.

Guided group support

Red Encourage children to consider how to guide the reader through the text and make the information easy to access (e.g. by using bulleted lists, emphasising headings and highlighting words).

Blue As for the red group. Encourage children to experiment with alternative layouts and fonts.

Yellow As for the red and blue groups. Encourage children to incorporate captioned illustrations and annotated diagrams.

Plenary Ask for volunteers to share their work, and invite positive comments from the class, focusing on aspects which should appeal to the given audience and which are particularly suitable for the given purpose. Discuss how best to publish the work in your chosen format. If it is to be a display, involve the children in decision-making about mounting and arranging the work. If it is to be a booklet, discuss what the cover should look like, and how all the writers will be acknowledged.

Homework suggestions

- Choose a topic that interests you. List what you know about it already and decide what else you would like to know. Make a list of questions and research them using four or five different reference resources. Keep notes of what you found out and where you found the information. **(After Session 1)**

- Create a glossary for an information text aimed at younger readers, making your explanations as clear as possible. **(After Session 1)**

- Choose an information text you have never read before. Read it carefully and identify whether the text is more characteristic of explanation or report. Copy out two passages of each text type. Annotate each passage to show the key features. **(After Session 2)**

- Ask a friend or family member to explain to you a process that they know well (e.g. how a car engine works, how yeast makes bread rise). Listen very carefully, ask questions and make notes. (Record the explanation on tape if you can!) Rewrite the explanation as a formal, impersonal text. Include extra information if you need to. What changes did you have to make in order to convert the spoken language to a written text? **(After Session 3)**

- Read and evaluate an information text. Identify the author and subject matter. Think about how much explanation and how much straightforward reporting the text contains. Look at the level of formality, and whether the language is impersonal or not. How clear and concise did you find the text? Prepare to tell the rest of the class about your findings. **(After Session 3)**

- Write a simple information text for a younger child. Write about something you know well – perhaps a hobby or special interest. Be sure to include elements of both report and explanation in order to inform your audience properly. **(After Session 4)**

- Find a very formal information text. Copy out part of it and highlight the elements that make it so formal. Now rewrite the text in an informal way, as if for one of your classmates. Remember that you still have to communicate the same information, and you still have to use subject-specific vocabulary. When you have finished, write a brief account of the changes you had to make. **(After Session 5)**

- Choose two information texts on the same subject but by different authors. Look carefully at the way each text is laid out and organised. Comment upon how helpful each text was and why. Make short lists of aspects that are most reader-friendly and features that caused problems or were unhelpful. **(After Session 7)**

UNIT 6 How to write explanations for different audiences and purposes

Colour the right number of stars to show how well you did the following things:

0 stars = I didn't do it.
1 star = I gave it a try.
2 stars = I did it quite well.

3 stars = I did it well.
4 stars = I did an excellent job!

I designed my own framework.	☆	☆	☆	☆
I composed a clear introduction which defined the subject.	☆	☆	☆	☆
I combined report and explanation text as required.	☆	☆	☆	☆
I organised my work into coherent, linked sections.	☆	☆	☆	☆
I wrote in the present tense throughout.	☆	☆	☆	☆
I wrote in an impersonal, formal style.	☆	☆	☆	☆
I used passive verbs.	☆	☆	☆	☆
I used technical and subject-specific vocabulary.	☆	☆	☆	☆

Something I am especially pleased with

Something my audience liked in my writing

Something I'd like to do better next time

How to write answers to SATs questions

The SATs section in the pupil's book (pages 68–75) provides typical sample SATs questions to which you may or may not want children to write full answers. The main purpose is to give children practice in how to approach a SATs writing question.

Here is some guidance on using the section in the pupil's book:

- Choose one of the SATs questions to work on.
- Read through it together in class.
- Give children 5–10 minutes, in pairs, to brainstorm answers to the questions on the form on page 68.
- Go through the children's answers together.

The following pages include some pointers as to the sort of answers children should be expected to come up with. You can photocopy these and hand them out to children for revision purposes.

1–2

Audience	No information given therefore assume teacher/marker
Purpose	To narrate imagined events To entertain, amuse or create suspense (various possible answers)
Text type	Story (question 2 demands specific genre: e.g. horror, science fiction, fairytale)
Structure	At least three main sections – beginning, middle and end – with the middle section subdivided into focused sections
Sequencing and linking in the text	Chronological sequence (but could include flashbacks)
Information and ideas	Make sure you cover the points listed in the question
Language	Language must be appropriate for the type of story/setting Include some powerful verbs and interesting descriptive language (including metaphors and similes if possible)
Star ways to impress the marker	★ Use paragraphs to set out ideas and events. ★ Choose appropriate vocabulary to give your story an authentic atmosphere. Use characteristic words and phrases from the genre. ★ Use sentences of different types and lengths to add interest. ★ Use a variety of time connectives. ★ Interweave elements of action, description and dialogue. ★ Think about using a flashback, or switching between settings.

3

Audience	Older children or teenagers
Purpose	To give personal details and information about the band To provide an accurate portrait of the character (and the setting) To offer an opinion about the person
Text type	Magazine report, probably including some elements of recount
Structure	An introductory section outlining the purpose of the interview A middle section, subdivided into paragraphs (e.g. about his home, the band's history, etc.) A final section, including a thought-provoking idea to leave readers thinking, or a 'scoop' revelation (e.g. the name of the band's new release)
Sequencing and linking in the text	Use informal sub-headings – perhaps questions, or exclamations Try to link one paragraph to the next in some way (e.g. asking a question in one paragraph which is answered in the next)
Information and ideas	The person – look, personality, clothes, behaviour The home – detailed, imaginative description The band – information as given in the fact boxes Opinions and personal observations from the reporter
Language	Informal, journalistic language Phrases older children or teenagers might use
Star ways to impress the marker	★ Include some direct quotes from your interview with Davie. ★ Use clearly organised paragraphs with headings in the style of a magazine. ★ Use language appropriate to the audience (including some trendy pop-scene words and phrases). ★ Use some journalistic words and phrases. ★ Use sentences of different types and lengths to vary the effect of the writing.

4

Audience	Mr and Mrs Fortunate
Purpose	To inform the family about what has happened To give key information about the holiday To raise enthusiasm – you really want the family to accept their prize, not turn it down
Text type	Letter Information Persuasion

Structure	Introductory section outlining the purpose of the letter
	Middle section organised into paragraphs giving information on:
	
	  O travel to the island
	  O some key attractions
	  O the hotel
	
	Final section, urging the family to take advantage of their good luck
	An appropriate closure

Sequencing and linking in the text	Opening statement prepares the way for description of the island Informal headings label the sections (possibly) Link phrases, leading questions or 'hooks' at the start or end of main sections
Information and ideas	Detailed descriptions of places and activities
Language	Conventional letter opening and closure Powerful 'fun' adjectives and verbs Holiday vocabulary Personal language (use 'you' and address the family directly)
Star ways to impress the marker	★ Use clearly organised paragraphs to set out ideas and information. ★ Consider use of headings. ★ Use characteristic holiday words and phrases. ★ Use some interesting similes/metaphors to describe the setting imaginatively. ★ Consider including a promotional slogan with alliteration or other word-play (e.g. using the name of the holiday company). ★ Use some questions and exclamations to establish a semi-formal 'chatty' tone to the letter. ★ Remember to use appropriate conventions to begin and end the letter.

5

Audience	Young adults
Purpose	To persuade people to choose a healthy lifestyle To give advice about what to do, and what not to do To warn about health and social problems resulting from bad lifestyle choices
Text type	Persuasive text
Structure	Opening section, setting out the point of view the leaflet promotes Middle section, either addressing a series of points raised by the 'unhealthy' group, and giving evidence against them *or* giving all the 'unhealthy' arguments followed by all the 'healthy' arguments Conclusion – why a healthy lifestyle is better
Sequencing and linking the text	Discussion connectives (e.g. *on the one hand/on the other hand, some people say/however*)
Information and ideas	Use as many as possible of the ideas in speech bubbles (plus ideas of your own)
Language	Informal language Powerful adjectives and verbs. Emotive, persuasive descriptions. Words which express strong disapproval of unhealthy behaviour and praise for healthy lifestyles
Star ways to impress the marker	★ Use clearly organised paragraphs to set out ideas and information. ★ Use a range of appropriate connectives. ★ Consider using bullet points, quotes or 'fact boxes' to make the leaflet look interesting. ★ Consider using a picture – indicate where this would go. ★ Include some persuasive catchphrases with alliteration or other word-play. ★ Use some questions and exclamations to involve the reader. ★ Think of a really powerful idea to leave the reader thinking about at the end.

6

Audience	Adult readers who know very little about the subject
Purpose	To give clear, accurate information about the game and the players
Text type	Report Explanatory text
Structure	Opening section, giving the name of the game and some basic facts about it Middle section, divided into smaller sections with sub-headings, giving further factual information Closing section (including a 'fascinating fact' if possible)
Sequencing and linking in the text	A sequence of sub-headings Chronological connectives in the explanation section Cause and effect connectives where appropriate
Information and ideas	Description of game, equipment, players Details of stages in the process of playing Personal opinions and comments (optional)
Language	Specific vocabulary relating to the game Chronological connectives (in explanation section) Cause and effect connectives Present tense verbs
Star ways to impress the marker	★ Include passive verbs in the explanation section. ★ Make your explanation clear for readers who are not familiar with the sport/game (e.g. explain any unfamiliar terms). ★ Use clearly organised paragraphs with logical headings to set out ideas and information. ★ Use a range of clear, chronological links between and within the paragraphs. ★ Suggest one or more useful diagrams/pictures (say briefly where they could go and what they would show).

7

Audience	Children of your age
Purpose	To give a detailed description of a place
Text type	Non-chronological report
Structure	Introduction, giving the name of the town or village and some key facts about it Main section, including several paragraphs with different focuses, organised logically, perhaps with sub-headings Closing section, giving one or more points of particular interest
Sequencing and linking in the text	Sub-headings to indicate structure Repeated use of town/village name
Information and ideas	Make sure you cover the points listed in the question
Language	Formal, impersonal style Present tense
Star ways to impress the marker	★ Use clearly organised paragraphs with logical headings. ★ Indicate any pictures, maps or photos that could be included and where these should be positioned. ★ Explain any names/words which would not be familiar to someone from outside your area.

8

Audience	Two children of your own age
Purpose	To give accurate facts about the show and the arrangements for the evening To describe the same event in two contrasting ways To persuade one reader to accept the invitation and the other to reject it
Text type	Letters Information and explanation Two different types of persuasion
Structure	An introductory section, saying why you're writing Several short sections of supporting information, referring to key features of the show (and what you are going to do that evening) A final section, urging the reader to accept (in one case) and trying to put them off (in the other case) An appropriate closure
Sequencing and linking in the text	Organise the middle section chronologically Include a range of time connectives within this section
Information and ideas	Detailed descriptions of the night out – who, what, where, when
Language	Powerful adjectives and verbs – with good or bad hints built in 'Warm' or 'cold' language to make each letter feel very different Tempting vocabulary for the first letter, offputting vocabulary for the second
Star ways to impress the marker	★ Use clearly organised paragraphs. ★ Use an informal, chatty style. ★ Make the two letters contrast strongly by using very different vocabulary for each. ★ Remember to use appropriate conventions to begin and end the letters.

Name

Date

Jim sets out to explore Treasure Island for the first time ...

I had crossed a marshy tract full of willows, bulrushes and odd, outlandish, swampy trees; and I had now come out upon the skirts of an open piece of undulating, sandy country, about a mile long, dotted with a few pines, and a great number of contorted trees, not unlike the oak in growth, but pale in the foliage, like willows. On the far side of the open stood one of the hills, with two quaint, craggy peaks, shining vividly in the sun.

I now felt for the first time the joy of exploration. The isle was uninhabited; my shipmates I had left behind, and nothing lived in front of me but dumb brutes and fowls. I turned hither and thither among the trees. Here and there were flowering plants, unknown to me; here and there I saw snakes, and one raised his head from a ledge of rock and hissed at me with a noise not unlike the spinning of a top. Little did I suppose that he was a deadly enemy, and that the noise was the famous rattle.

From *Treasure Island* by R.L. Stevenson

Name ....

Date ....

Beginning

Setting

Characters

Problem

Middle

Event 1

Event 2

Climax

End

Resolution

Name ....

Date ....

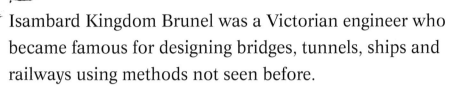

Isambard Kingdom Brunel was a Victorian engineer who became famous for designing bridges, tunnels, ships and railways using methods not seen before.

He was born in Portsmouth on 9th April 1806, the only son of Sophia Kingdom and Marc Isambard Brunel, a French engineer working in London.

When he was a child, Isambard first became interested in engineering and this was encouraged by his father. After attending school in England, he was sent to France where he learned more about being an engineer.

When Isambard was 16, he began working for his father, building the Thames Tunnel. Four years later he was placed in charge when his father became ill. During this time he was almost killed when the river burst into the tunnel, but he escaped with a broken leg. Unfortunately, six other workers were drowned.

After winning a competition for the best bridge design, Isambard began work on his famous Clifton Suspension Bridge. It took 30 years to build and is still used today. After this he built a railway line from London to Bristol on which Queen Victoria travelled – the first British monarch to travel by train. Finally he began building iron ships, eventually building the Great Britain and Great Eastern ships. Sadly, weak from years of hard work, he died on 15th September 1859.

Although Isambard Kingdom Brunel had critics, and not all his projects were successful, fellow engineer Daniel Gooch is recorded as saying "by his death the greatest of England's engineers was lost".

Name .... Date ....

Steven Spielberg has entertained many millions of people worldwide and is now considered to be the most successful film maker of all time.

Steven Allen Spielberg was born on 18th December 1946 in Cincinnati, Ohio, the first of Arnold and Leah Spielberg's four children. Little did they realise how famous he was to become. His first visit to the cinema at the age of six really excited him but, not long after, he began to develop a love of television. Despite his parents' attempts to control the children's viewing, he would sneak downstairs to watch when everyone was asleep.

Steven's experiences when he went to school were not always happy: being a slow reader and not good at games he began to feel rather isolated. At this time, his father was given an 8mm movie camera and, annoyed by his son's constant criticism, he handed Steven the camera, saying "Why don't you try?" After this, school life began to improve when Steven used his film making skills to feature a school bully in a star role.

A few years later, Steven began using his talent to make real films: *The Great Train Crash*, starring his own train set and *Firelight*, a science fiction film. He even managed to persuade the local airport to close a runway for the filming of this.

By the time he was twenty five, Spielberg was working on the moderately successful film *Duel*. Within five years, however, he was breaking box office records with *Jaws*, after which came many other film successes including *ET the Extraterrestrial* in the 1980s and, more recently, *Jurassic Park* and *Schindler's List*.

Spielberg is not without his critics. Some feel that his films lack artistic depth. No one, however, can deny his ability to control the emotions of his audience.

Name

Date

Questions	Answers (in note form)
Orientation (closed questions) Who? What? When? Why? Where?	
Key events (open questions) Question 1 Question 2 Question 3 Question 4	
Reorientation (open or closed question) Final question:	

Name
....

Date
....

SCHOOL REPORT FOR _____

DATE _____   YEAR GROUP _____   KEY STAGE _____

General progress:

English
Speaking and listening:

Reading:

Writing:

Curriculum Vitae

Name:

Date of birth:

Education:

Employment:

Personal interests:

Name ....

Date ....

What's in a mystery story?

? Mystery		Detective
Suspects	**Motives**	**Clues**
		Evidence

Mystery planning chart

Title: _____

Detective(s)	Mystery	Suspect 1
Name: Age: Character:		Name: Age: Character: Motive Clues
Clues		Suspect 2
		Name: Age: Character: Motive Clues
Final evidence	**Setting**	

Mystery planning chart   **Title:** _____

Detective	**Mystery**	**Suspect 2**
Name: Age: Character:		Name: Age: Character:
		Motive Clues
Clues	**Suspect 1**	**Suspect 3**
	Name: Age: Character:	Name: Age: Character:
	Motive Clues	Motive Clues
Red herring	**Setting**	
Final evidence	**Flashback setting**	

Name ....

Date ....

Title: _____

Beginning	Flashbacks
	Add more flashbacks below if you need them
Middle	
Climax	
End	

Name ....

Date ....

Use this framework to write another verse for 'The Charge of the Mouse Brigade'.

Claws _____ .

Claws _____ .

Claws _____ .

_____ .

Crash! – through the Catty flanks!

Captured _____ ,

Into _____ ,

Into _____ ,

Rode the Six Hundred.

Copymaster 13

Name .... Date ....

Underline the arguments **for** fox hunting in red and the arguments **against** fox hunting in green.

What is the main subject of each paragraph? Write this in the box on the left. The first one has been done for you.

Introduction Summary of issue	Should fox hunting be banned? Animal rights groups believe that fox hunting is a cruel sport. However, hunt supporters believe that fox hunting is fun and controls the number of foxes in the wild.
Paragraph 1 Cruelty	Hunters think that fox hunting is not cruel as the fox dies very quickly when the hounds catch it, but some research by animal rights groups shows that foxes suffer long and painful deaths when hounds attack them.
Paragraph 2	A report by the Countryside Alliance states that 15,900 people will lose their jobs if fox hunting is banned, although animal rights groups think that the actual number is no more than 700.
Paragraph 3	Hunt supporters believe that foxes are pests because they kill piglets and chickens on farms and they need to be hunted to be controlled. Animal rights groups think that hunting does not control the number of foxes and any foxes that kill piglets and chickens could be quickly shot.
Paragraph 4	Finally, fox hunting has been a sport in Britain for 200 years. Hunters think that if it is made illegal, a part of British life will be lost for ever. Animal rights groups think that fox hunting should be replaced by drag hunting, which means that the hounds chase a scent and do not kill foxes.

© Cambridge University Press 2001

Name .... Date ....

a Hunt supporters believe that foxes are pests and need to be hunted to be controlled. They state that farmers often call in the hunt to track down a fox that has been killing lambs, piglets or chickens.

b Animal rights groups propose that fox hunting be replaced by drag hunting, which involves the hounds chasing a scent and not killing animals.

c Pro-hunters think that fox hunting is not cruel as the fox dies very quickly when the hounds catch it.

d A report by the Countryside Alliance states that there are 15,900 people whose jobs directly depend on fox hunting. Consequently, if hunting is banned, all these people will be out of work. This will cause great hardship and distress to many families.

e However, some research shows that foxes suffer long and painful deaths when attacked by hounds.

f Finally, fox hunting has been a traditional sport in Britain for 200 years. Hunters think that if it is made illegal, a part of British culture will be lost for ever.

g While animal rights groups recognise that foxes can sometimes be pests, they think that hunting does not control the fox population. Any foxes that steal livestock could be shot. This would be a more effective, humane way of controlling foxes.

h Although anti-hunt campaigners acknowledge that some jobs will be lost, they state that the actual number is no more than 700.

Name ....

Date ....

Read this balanced report about tuna fishing.
Using the word banks below and some of your own ideas, list the missing words
and phrases.

Tuna fish live near dolphins. (**1**) _____ , tuna fishermen catch
dolphins in their nets. Laws have been passed to limit the number of dolphins that
die in this way. (**2**) _____ certain environmentalists believe that
no dolphins should die as a result of tuna fishing. (**3**) _____ ,
tuna fishermen think that a certain number of dolphin deaths is acceptable.

Environmentalists (**4**) _____ catching dolphins when fishing
for tuna will eventually endanger the species. No one knows exactly how many
dolphins die (**5**) _____ many of them are injured and die away
from the net. Fishermen (**6**) _____ dolphins are not
endangered and up to 3,000 per year can be killed without affecting the dolphin
population.

Environmentalists (**7**) _____ dolphins suffer slow, painful
deaths when trapped in fishing nets. (**8**) _____ fishermen
acknowledge that some dolphins do die in nets, they (**9**) _____
dolphins do not suffer unnecessarily, and many manage to escape.

Environmentalists (**10**) _____ all tuna fishing nets should be
banned and other methods of fishing introduced (**11**) _____
ending unnecessary dolphin deaths. (**12**) _____ , fishermen are
concerned about the effect of different forms of fishing on other sea life. They
(**13**) _____ sharks and turtles are now dying as a result,
(**14**) _____ endangering the survival of other species.

Connectives		Phrases to introduce points of view
because	consequently	are convinced that
however	similarly	argue that
thereby	therefore	believe that
whereas	while	think that
although	but	state that

Name ....   Date ....

Introduction (state position) *I believe that ...*	
Argument 1	**Point** **Evidence**
Argument 2	**Point** **Evidence**
Argument 3	**Point** **Evidence**
Argument 4	**Point** **Evidence**
Conclusion (summary and action)	

Name

Date

Title

1 Introduction (Summary of issue)		
	For	**Against**
2 Argument	Point Evidence	Point Evidence
3 Argument	Point Evidence	Point Evidence
4 Argument	Point Evidence	Point Evidence
5 Argument	Point Evidence	Point Evidence
6 Conclusion (Strengths and weaknesses)		

Name ....

Date ....

Title	Author

Reason for choosing book

	Beginning	Middle	End
Characters			
Plot			

What I liked best about the book	What I would change

Name

Date

   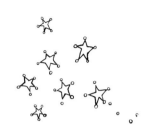

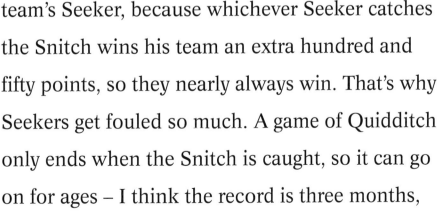

Wood reached into the crate and took out the fourth and last ball. Compared with the Quaffle and the Bludgers, it was tiny, about the size of a large walnut. It was bright gold and had little fluttering silver wings.

"*This*," said Wood, "is the Golden Snitch, and it's the most important ball of the lot. It's very hard to catch because it's so fast and difficult to see. It's the Seeker's job to catch it. You got to weave in and out of the Chasers, Beaters, Bludgers and Quaffle to get it before the other team's Seeker, because whichever Seeker catches the Snitch wins his team an extra hundred and fifty points, so they nearly always win. That's why Seekers get fouled so much. A game of Quidditch only ends when the Snitch is caught, so it can go on for ages – I think the record is three months, they had to keep bringing on substitutes so the players could get some sleep."

From *Harry Potter and the Philosopher's Stone* by J.K. Rowling

Name ....

Date ....

A scarlet steam engine was waiting next to a platform packed with people. A sign overhead said *Hogwarts Express, 11 o'clock.* Harry looked behind him and saw a wrought-iron archway where the ticket box had been, with the words *Platform Nine and Three-Quarters* on it. He had done it.

Smoke from the engine drifted over the heads of the chattering crowd, while cats of every colour wound here and there between their legs. Owls hooted to each other in a disgruntled sort of way over the babble and the scraping of heavy trunks. The first few carriages were already packed with students, some hanging out of the window to talk to their families, some fighting over seats. Harry pushed his trolley off down the platform in search of an empty seat. He passed a round-faced boy who was saying, "Gran, I've lost my toad again."

Name ....

Date ....

BOOM.

The whole shack shivered and Harry sat bolt upright, staring at the door. Someone was outside, knocking to come in.

BOOM. They knocked again. Dudley jerked awake.

"Where's the cannon?" he said stupidly.

There was a crash behind them and Uncle Vernon came skidding into the room. He was holding a rifle in his hands – now they knew what had been in the long, thin package he had brought with them.

"Who's there?" he shouted. "I warn you – I'm armed!"

There was a pause. Then –

SMASH!

The door was hit with such force that it swung clean off its hinges and with a deafening crash landed flat on the floor.

A giant of a man was standing in the doorway. His face was almost completely hidden by a long, shaggy mane of hair and a wild, tangled beard, but you could make out his eyes, glinting like black beetles under all the hair.

The giant squeezed his way into the hut, stooping so that his head just brushed the ceiling. He bent down, picked up the door and fitted it easily back into its frame. The noise of the storm outside dropped a little. He turned to look at them all.

"Couldn't make us a cup o' tea, could yeh? It's not been an easy journey ..."

From *Harry Potter and the Philosopher's Stone* by J.K. Rowling

PUBLISHED BY THE PRESS SYNDICATE OF THE UNIVERSITY OF CAMBRIDGE
The Pitt Building, Trumpington Street, Cambridge, United Kingdom

CAMBRIDGE UNIVERSITY PRESS
The Edinburgh Building, Cambridge CB2 2RU, UK
40 West 20th Street, New York, NY 10011-4211, USA
10 Stamford Road, Oakleigh, VIC 3166, Australia
Ruiz de Alarcón 13, 28014 Madrid, Spain
Dock House, The Waterfront, Cape Town 8001, South Africa

http://www.cambridge.org

© Cambridge University Press 2001

First published 2001
Reprinted 2001

Printed in the United Kingdom by GreenShires Group Ltd, Kettering, Northamptonshire.

Typefaces Concorde, Frutiger, ITC Kabel   *System* QuarkXPress®

A catalogue record for this book is available from the British Library

ISBN 0 521 80553 8

Cover design by Traffika Publishing Ltd
Design by Peter Simmonett and Angela Ashton
Artwork chosen by Heather Richards
Illustrations by James Bartholomew/Heather Richards, Eikon Illustration, Sam Hearn/Eastwing,
Sally Kindberg, Janet Simmonett, Ron Tiner

We would like to thank the following teachers and headteachers for their help on Cornerstones for
Writing: Anne Allen, Lorna Ferry, Bonnie Kennedy, Jackie Lucas, Carol Meek and Susan Seed.